An Intricate Dance:

Stepparents Tell Us How They Found Their Rhythm

Susan Philips

AYWN PUBLICATIONS
Portland, Oregon

An Intricate Dance: Stepparents Tell Us How They Found Their Rhythm

Email for more information:
fran@aywnpublications.com

ISBN: 978-1-893471-24-5

Library of Congress Control Number: 2013930397

1. Stepparents 2. Parents

2. Families 4. Divorce

Published in the United States by AYWN Publications, Portland, OR

Cover art by Anita Jones, Another Jones Graphics, Portland, OR

I dedicate this book to Art, my husband
and my son Jake's stepfather, who continues to be
Jake's biggest cheerleader.

Acknowledgments

I begin by thanking the stepparents I interviewed for allowing me to tell their stories. It wasn't easy, not for any of them. Yet they kept at it, and for that I am grateful.

I want to thank Cathryn Bond Doyle, the founder of Stepmoms on a Mission (www.smoms.org), for her time, generosity and most of all, for her wise counsel.

I want to thank Frances Caldwell, my editor, publisher and friend for giving me the chance to follow my dreams. To all of you out there who would like to write a book, I advise you to find your Fran Caldwell.

And as always, I want to thank my family. Like other stepparents in this book, my husband and I stayed together and have now become grandparents. We could not have done this but for the support and love of our families.

Table of Contents

Stepparent Workshop Guide

Introduction

"When you marry someone with children, you do not begin with a clean slate," my counselor reminded my husband and me early on in our marriage as we were struggling to create our new stepfamily. "Quite the contrary," she continued. "You will be sharing your bed with a lot of new people, so you better make sure it's big enough." Trust me, that was an image I could have lived without. But she had a point. When you marry someone with children, in an instant, you inherit a ton of new people—ex-husbands, ex-wives, grandparents, brothers and sisters, uncles, aunts and even neighbors and friends. It seems that everyone has an opinion about your new marriage, and an even stronger one about how you should treat the kids. And you can forget those long walks on the beach with your new spouse where you slowly get to know each other. Gone. Your life becomes one big organizational chart. So I was not at all surprised when in our last session, our therapist left us with these "hopeful" words: "Stepfamilies are hard, and sometimes, love is not enough."

Love is not enough? What was she talking about? After all, I had grown up with a mom whose daily mantra was "If you love someone, everything will work out." But even she had her doubts when I told her I was about to marry someone with three kids. "Really," she said, "you might want to reconsider." Thankfully over time, those three kids, and the fact that my own son seemed pretty happy, completely won over her and my father. But there were many days, especially at the beginning of our marriage, when I too wondered if love would be enough.

If love is not enough, what is? What can parents and stepparents, the adults in the situation, do to create both a happy new marriage and happy stepchildren? And how long will it take to get there? Important questions for sure, since the divorce rate for second marriages with children is a whopping 70 percent; this is 20 percent higher than the rate for first marriages. We may want to rethink what we mean by "family values." But forever the optimist, I was encouraged by the fact that 30 percent of stepfamilies do not end in divorce. I wondered, what do stepfamilies that stay together do differently than those that do not? What can we learn from both?

Several years ago, I asked these questions to ten now-grown stepchildren for my book *Stepchildren Speak: Ten Grown-up Stepchildren Teach Us How to Build Healthy Stepfamilies*. In my discussions with the stepchildren, I learned a number of things. The most obvious—kids do not want to be stepchildren. They would prefer to be living with their "real" parents. Stepparents are the symbol of the hard, cold fact that their parents are no longer married. And as much as the stepchildren may like and in some cases even grow to love their stepparents, their initial feeling is "Why are you here?" I also learned, contrary to popular opinion, none of the stepkids wanted to hate their stepparents. In their heart of hearts, they wanted to have a loving relationship with them. They wanted their stepparents to take an interest in their lives, cheer for them at their baseball games, talk with their teachers at back-to-school nights, take them to their doctor appointments—all the things parents routinely do. On the other hand, as much as they wanted their stepparents to participate in their lives, they did not want them to try and take the place of their *real* mom or dad. The stepchildren wanted their *real* parents to remain their parents, and they wanted their stepparents to become parent-like. They did not want them to ever cross this line. On this point they were crystal clear.

Fair enough. But then it occurred to me, were their stepparents as crystal clear on this point? Did they understand the distinction between parent and parent-like? We assume that stepparents will magically know what to do. But when you think about it, why would they? Where would they learn this? Most of us go on instinct, thinking that if we love kids and kids love us, we'll do just fine. We'll be great stepparents. And then reality sets in, problems begin to emerge, and we find ourselves staring at the ceiling in the middle of the night thinking, "I have absolutely no idea what to do. What is my role in this family? Help."

In searching for answers, some people turn to advice books, others to counselors, and still others to chocolate. All good ideas for sure, especially the chocolate. But there is another place to turn, one we often overlook, and that is to the people who have experienced it up close and personal—stepparents themselves. How did they figure out their role? What advice can other stepparents offer to get through those sleepless nights? And while it goes without saying that every experience is different, taken as a whole, their advice can yield important lessons about how to build a successful stepfamily.

It wasn't hard to find stepparents who wanted to share their experiences. It turns out there are a lot of stepparents who want and in some cases need to tell their stories. "This is a lot cheaper than therapy," one of the stepparents told me after our first interview. My biggest questions: How do I pick the people? What kind of "criteria" should I use? Daunting questions for sure since the universe of stepfamilies is so enormous. The fact is that there are now more people living in stepfamilies than in intact ones, so finding anything close to a "representative sample" is impossible.

At the end of the day, the most important thing was to find people who were thoughtful, interesting, and had something useful to say. I think I succeeded. Soon you will meet them. Five are stepmoms and four are stepdads. Some grew up in stepfamilies, and others did not. Some have wonderful things to say about their experiences, and others not so much. Some are still in the throes of trying to establish their stepfamilies, and others have stayed together long enough to have grandkids. They are a wonderful mix of personalities, backgrounds, and experiences, and it is my hope and theirs that you learn as much as you can, whether positive or negative, so that you will be a little more prepared when you take on this role. You may not see yourself in every story, but I assure you, you will learn something from each.

Sarah's Story

Sarah married Ed in her late thirties. Ed has two children from his first marriage, a girl, Taylor, and a boy, David. Together they have one son, Jake.

What does family mean to you?

Family means warmth, tradition, and acceptance of eccentricities.

I come from what I consider to be a traditional family. I have two older sisters. I have loving parents. I have a very hardworking, entrepreneurial dad who I think hung the moon and probably some of the stars also. My dad is such a great guy that when my maternal grandmother passed away when I was a girl, it was my dad who convinced my mother that her father should move in with us. My grandfather spent years with us until he decided that there was a better place to spend the winter. I grew up in the kind of family where you squeezed in and made room, and where there were older sisters to bash on you, but they would stand up for you if somebody else came abashing. My mother worked part-time outside of the home, but she could cook and bake and do it all, and have every kind of family event and never forget a birthday. That's what I mean by tradition and warmth and acceptance of little oddities and quirks.

Both my father's and mother's grandparents were immigrants. I have the kind of family where the lines are fuzzy between sides of the family. My dad and mom each had two siblings. Most of my cousins are people I am in touch with regularly. Even though we didn't live close by, there was just warmth that existed, and the door was open, the smile was there when you came in, and food in the freezer if it wasn't already on the table. If there is a family event, my father's cousins are excited to see my mother's cousins. There is no "these are my people and those are your people." I attribute this to my mom and her mother's sense of family, and the fact that for my mother everyone was welcome. There was always room at the table. I couldn't believe how difficult it was to find someone I was sure shared my idea of family. It took me a long time to find the right guy.

Meeting my future husband

I had always hoped I would meet someone, but I had gotten to a place in life where I realized that if I didn't, I was going to be okay. I had an apartment in downtown Portland that I loved. I had friends. I had activities. I was involved in my community, and I was on the board of a local charity. I had a full and busy life. I wasn't sitting in my apartment hoping that the pizza delivery guy was going to be the one.

I was in my upper thirties when I met Ed. On our first date Ed told me he had been divorced for five years and had two children. I thought, "Here is a guy who isn't nursing divorce hurt." Because his ex-wife was married, she wasn't calling him in the middle of the night to fix a broken light. And I said to myself, "I have nephews and nieces. I like kids, and kids like me." And because this man was open to having another child, this was not someone who was going to say, "I've got my kids; if you want to be with me you have to subordinate a life goal."

Ed told me he was looking to get married again and have a family, and I thought, "That's refreshing. How many guys have I dated where it took months before I finally got out of them that they weren't looking for a permanent relationship, much less marriage?" We went out on a couple of dates, and then my grandfather passed away. I was heartsick. My grandfather was the guy who was waiting at the top of the driveway when I came home from school every day. I kind of went into hibernation, and then a friend told me that my grandfather would not want me to be sitting at home on weekend nights. I called Ed and told him that I was sorry I hadn't returned his calls, that my grandfather had died and that I had just been knocked for a loop. He said, "I really understand. My grandmother lived with us when I was growing up, and I remember when she passed away how absolutely devastated I was." And that was it. I said to myself, "We may not agree on everything in the world, but there is some element of family that he and I are both tuned into the same way."

Meeting Taylor and David, Ed's kids

I wanted to make sure that I was in love with Ed and he was in love with me before I met his children. I didn't want to get involved with anybody's kids until I was certain that I was really in love with their father. We must have gone out for four or five months before I met his kids, who were at that time ten and fourteen and living in the suburbs. Because I fancied myself a super auntie, and I was a cool cousin to the children of all of my older cousins, I assumed I was just going to love his kids and they were going to love me

The first time we met we went to a show in the city. Then we went to a funky, retro, vinyl, rock-and-roll restaurant, off the beaten path, very not like Ed. I picked it purposely. I knew it was a cool place for a teenager to go, not like a chain restaurant. I knew it presented me as being different, not just some lady in the suburbs. I thought this gave us an opportunity to have a meal, go to a show, talk a little after, and then go our separate ways. It had a definitive stop and start. This is good advice. Make sure that the first meeting has a plan, an entrance and exit strategy, and a parameter of time so that it doesn't become "does she stay over or not?"

The first meeting was lovely. It was exactly as Ed said it would be. He told me, "David will be great. He'll love you. Taylor will be as polite and pleasant and wonderful as can be, and she will want information from you, but anything you say will go back to her mother." Taylor showed me pictures of her friends but also pictures of her mother and stepdad. She was letting me know that mom and stepdad were right up there with her friends. She totally matched Ed's description. She wasn't unpleasant that day, but there was no warmth. The knife was always there.

Ed's divorce

Ed and his ex were married for fourteen years, from "I do" to when the judge said, "It's officially over." The kids were five and eight when they divorced. They shared parenting of the children. Ed had at least two dinners a week and every other weekend with his kids; however, his ex would always refer to his time with the kids as "visitation." There was stupid, unnecessary bad blood.

Ed was never stingy with anything. If there was a sweatshirt to be purchased, he gave money. He never said no. He gave her carte blanche to pay for their son's bar mitzvah. It blew me away that we paid for her friends and family to come to the bar mitzvah. I would never think of asking someone to pay for my friends. This is about my sense of what is fair. But Ed never said a bad word about his ex-wife.

When Ed and his ex sold their house, he moved into his parents' house and she moved into her parents' house until she remarried. My in-laws told me a story about something that happened while Ed was living with them. They were sitting around the dining room table, and his son David said, "I have a new daddy." My father-in-law said in a calm and polite manner, "No, you have one dad and that is Ed. Your mom is married to Phil and he is your stepdad. It's great that your mom is happy, but Ed is your father." Taylor immediately called her mother to tell her what was said. When Ed got on the phone, his ex screamed at him. My hunch is that somewhere in David's mind this experience stuck. I have had a recounting of this story many times.

During the time Ed's ex lived with her parents, who were not the warmest most loving people to Ed, the grandmother and mother probably bashed and trashed him in front of his daughter who sat there and absorbed it all. Before the divorce, Taylor and Ed had a loving relationship. Her anger was a reflection of her mom's attitudes and probably her mom's inability to take any of the blame for the breakup of the marriage. Whether the marriage was good, bad, or indifferent was irrelevant. Clearly, she painted herself as the victim, and so Taylor also painted herself as a victim of awful Ed.

When Ed and I were engaged, a book about parental alienation came out called *Divorce Poison*. I remember we were driving in the car, and I was reading it out loud. He kept saying, "Stop," and he would complete the sentence, or tell a story that was reflective of what the book said. What it said was that girls of a certain age tend to respond differently than boys to this tremendous upheaval, divorce. For girls of eight and nine years, prepuberty, their mother is their role model.

Marriage and stepkids

I knew the kids about a year before we got married: six months of being dad's girlfriend and six months of being dad's fiancée. Ed was hoping that I was going to help create this pleasant, conflict-free, diversionary experience. He was kind of clueless about how his own behavior allowed things to keep happening and didn't know how to set any parameters with his daughter. It was crazy land, so we saw a counselor for awhile before the wedding. The counseling was very helpful and gave me a chance to be heard. The counselor said my concerns were realistic. But counseling wasn't really enough.

My stepson David was ecstatic about our getting married. At the wedding, my father welcomed the kids into the family. He told them that change can be upsetting but it can also bring new things. My father had David at "welcome to the family."

It's amazing how much positive I have had from David, but how little airtime this gets in a conversation about being a stepmom. I would like to think that a lot of kids are like David, open and receptive to having someone new in their lives, someone who can bring something different from what already exists.

I was fortunate that while Ed and I were dating and

newly wed I still had my apartment in the city, so the city became a special thing for David and me. We would take the train to Chinatown and eat dim sum and have bubble tea. We ate the kind of things my husband wouldn't eat. I can't say enough about how important it is to find a little patch of earth that you and your stepkid can share that doesn't belong to anyone else. It is really important for stepparents to present themselves as something different, not better, but someone who brings a different outlook, perspective and opportunities. I put in my head that Ed's ex-wife could have the town where she lived, but I would have Portland and the rest of the world. I could show the kids things she couldn't.

David and I had lots of special time together and still do. One of these times came on a Friday night when Taylor was out with her friends. He was around twelve. We were goofing around making chocolate chip cookies, pretending that we were on the food channel, and I jokingly said, "Ed, get out the video camera; we're on television." David and I did an entire batch of cookies as if he was the food chef and I was his assistant. To this day we watch this video.

David and I used to go biking together, and we would often make a pit stop at Ed's parents' house. When David got old enough, he started making the stops on his own. My in-laws say this was so important in the development of their relationship with David because it allowed him to relate to the family without Taylor being there. When she was around, he always walked on egg shells and was constantly doing that "eye check" with her. I am sure that he knew that whatever was said would be reported to base camp.

When Ed and I were expecting a baby, we didn't tell anybody except my mother and my in-laws until we told David and Taylor. We didn't want them to find out from anyone else. We told David together and Ed told Taylor separately. We promised David, who was fourteen at the time, that the little kid coming wasn't changing the pecking order of things, and that it wasn't going to become all about the baby. We told him that once the child was born, he would have twenty to twenty-five years of hero worship. David was in the waiting room when I delivered, and he stayed with us for the first week after I came home from the hospital, which either puts me up for stepmom of the century, or crazy woman of the year. After the baby was born, Taylor didn't stay with us another weekend.

The bond was always there with David. I remember when we packed up my apartment, I said to him, "Please pack these nicely because they will be your first set of dishes and glasses." He knew that I knew that this was my stuff for him to enjoy. I remember the first time we said I love you to each other. I was in tears I was so happy. Now David lives in an apartment in the city with a ton of guys. When they needed furniture, I went to my favorite close-out place and found all kinds of great stuff, and Ed, our son Jake, and I drove the furniture to David's new apartment. When we got there, I sat down on one of the chairs to rest, and it broke. It only had three legs. We could laugh at this together.

From the beginning, I knew my stepdaughter Taylor and I wouldn't be close. Right after Ed and I got married, Taylor laid one of those "you're not my mother" things on me. I told her, "I am certainly not, but I am your father's wife, and I should be treated in a respectful and polite manner." She walked off. What could she say?

For awhile things got better. Ed was able to set standards of behavior. Taylor was warming up. A new pattern had started to develop, and her mother could smell it. Taylor's loyalty was about to be tested. Of course, she should be loyal to her mother, but I could tell that a light switch had been turned on, and then we got pretty much non-stop nasty Taylor. She began to believe that her mom's universe was the good universe and anything else was the dark side.

For example, when Taylor was sixteen, we gave her a cell phone. I was in a cool part of Portland one night and gave her a call. I said, "I see fun shops and great stuff here. We have to come back on the weekend and go to some of these stores." She asked, "Why are you calling me?" It was as though I was wasting her few available minutes.

On another occasion Taylor came to our house to do something with Ed. When they finished, he was supposed to do something with me and Jake. It was taking a lot longer than it was supposed to, so after about forty-five minutes, I told them that Jake and I were going to go to Ed's parents' house. Taylor flew off the handle, yelling and screaming. I told her that she was in my home and had to be respectful to me. She said, "This is not your house," and I told her that if she felt that way, she could go to town hall and check out the records. Ed told her, "You have to go. If you can't be respectful, you have to leave."

I could not deal with the lack of respect. I could deal with the fact that the bed wasn't made. I could deal with the dirty dishes in the sink and a lot of other things. You don't have to like me, but you gotta treat me with respect and dignity, *especially in my own home.* As long as Taylor is polite and pleasant to me in my own home, in front of Jake, her half brother, she can *think* whatever she wants, but she better stuff a sock into it. That's it. That is all I ask.

I have learned from this that if a person isn't open to a relationship, it's not going to happen. Some relationships are just not meant to be forever, or just not at this time. You could stand on your head, you could be the personal assistant of Justin Bieber, and your stepdaughter may still not like you. It's like the Herman's Hermits song, "Henry the 8th, I am." You have to get to a place where you realize that each verse is the same as the first, and then not die a thousand deaths over stuff that is just happening over and over.

Now Taylor has a nice relationship with Ed, and she is warm and pleasant with me. She even called me on Mother's Day. I used to live wanting a warm relationship for her and me, but now I live in the moment. If it's good, I'm happy. If I feel it's self-serving on her part, I laugh, or I call some friends who "get it." You change, evolve. You have to. Maybe with maturity you get to a place where you lose the bitterness and you realize it's not all about you and you get a better perspective. I totally wish her the best, and I really hope that some day we will have an amazing, great relationship. But the ball is in her court. I'll extend olive branches the rest of my life. This is my hopeful but realistic attitude toward my stepdaughter.

Reflections

The first few years of my marriage I felt tense. I felt

anxious. I felt a lack of control. I hate using that word. *Control* sounds like you want to be controlling, like all the things the wicked stepmother gets saddled with. I always thought that being a grown-up is gaining control over your life and your choices. That is so much a part of growing up, being the one who calls the shots. Then suddenly you find yourself in a situation where there seems to be a trump card. Somebody gets an unlimited quantity in their hand to play over and over again. It's the lack of control over what you are going to do on the weekends, how you are going to spend your money, how you are going to be treated in your own home, and on and on. You go from being a great savior who's going to make it better, and then you feel as if you're falling into shrill-harpy territory. It was very hard. It was very hard. I always wanted to find a way to make things work. It wasn't a pretty time. It left its mark.

What then is the proper role of the stepmother? Each situation is unique because of the players involved, but think about that word *step.* You're going to *step* up at times and do so much for the family; you're going to *step* back sometimes when you really think that someone should pat you on the back and say thank you, but nobody does. You are also going to be *stepped* on.

My number-one piece of advice is that you gotta figure out what you want to fall on your sword over. When you're young you are willing to fight a thousand fights, and you're willing to die a thousand deaths. So many things matter. Being a stepparent can be the most important lesson in figuring out what *really* matters. I'm not going to get my knickers in a twist when my stepkids leave their wet towels on the floor or food in their bedrooms, take cookies into the den, forget to use a coaster, or any of the other crap that I think becomes unnerving to many stepparents. At the end of the day, you are fighting over silly turf. You have to get to a place where you say, "I'm only going to worry about the big picture. I'm going to let a lot of the little stuff go."

I have also learned that you can't take on your husband's battles as your own. I think that is something a lot of stepmoms do. You love your spouse. You want your spouse to have a wonderful relationship with his children. The next thing you know you're in conflict with someone with whom you have no reason to be in conflict. Until you have a reason, stay out of it. Trust me; there will be a reason if the ex is difficult and mean-spirited. Until then you don't have to grab on to your spouse's battles.

Another lesson I learned about being a stepmom is not to get on other people's crazy trains. There are so many times you make yourself sick by ruminating. Once you have identified that there is crazy behavior, and once you have batted it around your head a few times, like the Herman's Hermits song, you are crazy to continue to expect sanity. Once you have accepted this, crazy can actually be a little funny. For example, instead of getting upset when you pull up to the curb to pick up the kids and mom or stepdad closes the blinds in the living room as if you were going to peer in and see some secret, you can laugh at it. It bothers you less. It got me to a place where I could say, "I don't really care what they think of me."

It really helps if you've got your cadre of close amigas that you can call up and vent, let it rip, get it over with, have a good chuckle, and move on. There are so many different challenges that stepmoms have. Some stepmoms are dealing with ungrateful, clingy or annoying stepkids. Others can't get through to their stepkids. Others feel like James the Chauffeur. Everyone has a different thing, but everyone lives in this confusing universe where they feel overwhelmed, lonely, anxious, and down in the dumps. The only way they can get air is to scream.

My final thought is that when you contemplate becoming a stepparent, realize that the relationship never begins on a completely secure footing. First, you must figure out exactly what it is that you bring to the party, and exactly what you want out of this relationship. If you can get your adult priorities straight and draw your boundaries, then you might not end up doing the same things again and again like in the Herman's Hermits rule of stepparenting.

Harry and Joan's Stories

When Harry and Joan married, he had three daughters, Karen, Charity, and Maggie from his first marriage, and she had four children, three sons, Thomas, Bob and Jared and a daughter, Lilly, from two previous marriages. They have no children together.

Harry's Story

What does family mean to you?

Anyone that is part of your home is your family. In our case, we have kids from both families who live in our home. I think of all of them as family.

Growing up

When I was a kid there was less confusion about who might or might not be a part of the family. It was a very standard "Dad, Mom, and the kids" situation. Later, my grandmother lived with us for several years, so the idea of having someone in your home who was not part of the "normal" family unit became more familiar. There are five kids in my family. I am the oldest, and then girl, boy, girl, boy. My mother was a stay-at-home mom until the children were mostly grown.

I grew up in Utah from the time I was five until I went to college. When I was too young to remember we moved around a lot because my father was in the military, but I went to the same school from the middle of kindergarten through the time I graduated from high school. The high school was in a neighboring town because that's the only way they could get enough kids to form a high school. We lived in a rural town of 2,000 people. A significant majority of the people in that town were LDS (Latter Day Saints), and a lot of the social activities revolved around the church congregation. One night a week I was at the church building, theoretically for Boy Scouts, but mostly we just played basketball. But every guy in the neighborhood knew that was where to go if you wanted to hang out with anyone that night. We went to church every Sunday, and the church would frequently sponsor a dinner or potluck that would be one of the social events of the neighborhood. School and church were the two main things people did.

I always thought I would have a family and raise kids. I wasn't really sure about a career. I went into science and got a BS in physics. It wasn't till after graduation that I got interested in business and wound up with an MBA. That has guided my career ever since. For the past several years I have worked in banking.

Mary, wife one

After I came back from my LDS mission to the Philippines, I returned to college and lived in an apartment complex just off campus. Some of the people in that complex, including my ex, had also gone on a mission to the same country. That's how I met my ex. She was the first person I was serious about after I came back from being a missionary. While there's no rule about it or anything, in Mormon culture, after you have gone on a mission, everyone assumes that your next order of business is to start serious dating and then get married. It's kind of a rite of passage.

That expectation really influenced my decision to get married. It wasn't something I planned for as a goal, but something that presented itself and I thought, "This is what comes next. I'm back from my mission and I should start dating." This was followed immediately by, "Now that I'm dating, I should get engaged." It was a momentum type situation. I think I was genuinely very naïve about relationships and dating. We dated awhile, got engaged, and got married. I can remember sitting at my parents' house and my sisters saying, "So, are you going to get engaged?" And I remember thinking, "Yes, that's what comes next. I guess I should do it."

When we first got married we talked about not having kids right away. That didn't last—we were married for less than a year when a switch went off in Mary's head, and she decided she really wanted children sooner. We debated the question, and I lost. So we started having kids before I graduated and soon after she graduated, so she didn't ever really work. I think the reason she started looking to get married was she was getting to an age where most of her peers were married, and the reason she started having kids was because a lot of our friends were and she felt that if she didn't start soon, she would miss out. Social pressure played a big role in her decisions.

We had three kids in about five years. I wanted to have them close together, which is similar to my family, and once we started I wanted to have that phase of our lives done before we were too old. I wanted to have the kids grown up and out on their own so I could keep going forward with life and still have plenty of life to live. I like the idea of being grandpa and grandma, living in a smaller apartment, doing our own thing while we're still not on oxygen.

We were married over ten years. Mary stayed home with the kids and I worked. At the time, I would have rated it as a good marriage, but now, having a different standard to compare it to, I would rate it below average. I didn't have a clear picture of what a marriage should be. We didn't know how to communicate. I grew up thinking that if there was tension you just walked away and came back later and pretended there wasn't anything wrong. I think that contributed to a build-up of dissatisfaction on both our parts. I don't think this is the healthiest dynamic obviously, but that is what I thought you did.

Divorce

Divorce was Mary's idea. She had met someone online. I guess I should say she hadn't actually met him physically yet, but she decided she was in love and was going to leave me. She didn't know anything about him. I think this was just an excuse to get out of the marriage, really. We saw a marriage counselor through our church but that didn't make much difference. Meanwhile she kept quietly pursuing this online guy and started an affair. I finally threw in the towel.

We had joint custody, not quite 50/50 at first. Over time the disparity has grown and she has the majority of the custody time now. I tried to provide as much stability and continuity as I could. We both agreed to stay nearby so the kids could stay at the same school, and I tried to arrange things with my work schedule so if I had them on a school day I would be able to get them off to school before I went to work. The problem was that in practice "providing stability" turned out to mean that whatever their mom wanted she got, whether it was a change in schedule, money to pay for clothes, whatever. I was so focused on stability that I went along without making waves, which in hindsight created a power dynamic I now regret.

I tried to keep things looking smooth, on the outside at least, but the flip side of that coin is that I don't know that the children really dealt with the divorce emotionally. We maintained this illusion that there wasn't any issue or conflict or anything to worry about, so when we were unable to maintain that any longer it was actually harder for the kids. It's one thing to want to be as smooth as possible; it's another thing to try and mask the reality of life from them. If I could send a message back to myself it would be "This is not sustainable. You cannot keep this mirage up forever."

As I moved forward in my life and started having obligations of my own, suddenly there was conflict. Now I couldn't keep doing everything their mother wanted. I had my own obligations that I hadn't had before, and I started saying "no" sometimes. That change seemed to surprise my ex, and it created a lot of conflict that we are still dealing with.

Stephen R. Covey in his book *The Seven Habits of Highly Effective People* writes that independence has to come before interdependence. If you don't move through independence you become codependent. I think this also applies to building households. You go from dependent when you are one household, and you have to evolve into two independent households if you want to be interdependent. Co-parenting or some of the other things that are popular rely on the independence of the two parents. If you have too much involvement with each other, or one parent taking control of both homes, you can't develop the interdependent relationship that people want. It's not co-parenting if one parent gets their way all the time.

By the time we were actually divorced, I was emotionally done with the idea of being married. But I let myself stay entangled for the sake of the girls. That was the magic phrase: "for the girls." As in, go buy these clothes "for the girls." Do extra driving during my time "for the girls." If it was "for the girls," I would do it. She played on my guilt and my desire to provide for my kids and had me dancing like a puppet on a string. She managed to get a new computer, help in moving from one apartment to another and anything else she wanted by telling me it was "for the girls." That caused an unhealthy situation. I didn't like her or want to talk to her, but if the phone rang and I saw it was my ex, I would drop what I was doing and pick it up because it might be "for the girls."

As men, we tend not to give ourselves enough credit for knowing what our children need. We believe the story that mom knows best, so we allow ourselves to be the implementer of mom's will regarding the children. If mom says they need it, they must need it. The advice I would give is to simply give yourself a little credit for knowing your children. If you think that the kids need something, then do it, but don't automatically assume that the kids need it because your ex says they do. You can do anything you want "for the girls" as long as it's what you want to do and not what your ex is telling you to do. If you're making your own decisions regarding your children's welfare, you're becoming that independent household they need. If you find there is a co-parenting arrangement that works for you, great. But you have to do this on your own two feet. You have to be a parent of your own accord. No kid needs "mom" and "mom's babysitter." If you're going to be involved, be a great father and do it for yourself and your children, not for your ex.

Meeting my present wife, Joan

Joan and I met on an online dating site targeting people from our religion. I had been dating for two years or so, but most of the people I dated did not meet my kids. Things happened really fast with Joan. We dated from February to May before we got engaged and married in July, which is just rocket fast.

I was a little bit intimidated by the new family at first because seven is a lot of kids. The thing that had me nervous was the sheer complexity of going from a medium-size family to an enormous family. The number of kids and the responsibility of a family that big were intimidating to me. I love Joan and I love her kids, but adjusting to the new family dynamic and learning new quirky family habits were daunting.

On top of that, shortly before I met Joan, I had to make a work decision. My department was being moved to Chicago, and I could either relocate or get a severance package and stay in Utah. I chose to move to Chicago. I had always wanted to live in a big city, and also I needed a separation from the divorced-parent scene. Being constantly under my ex's supervision was wearing me down, but I could not admit it at the time. So instead, I decided to move, and I convinced myself I could have this great new relationship with my kids. They could come to visit in the summer or Christmas breaks, and we could do cool things in the city. I wanted a new way of doing things and I thought relocating was my ticket out. My move to Chicago turned out to be great for my relationship with Joan. We were discovering shared interests. Joan had never been to a big city before and liked seeing the city architecture, going to plays, and just watching the hustle and bustle of a big city, things I probably wouldn't have spent as much time noticing without her. We were discovering new things together.

One great thing I didn't expect was that there was no baggage associated with this new experience. Chicago didn't have any of my history or her history, so nothing we were doing reminded us of our exes. We were lucky because we had Chicago, but I think any couple could find something like that no matter where they are. Maybe you take up scuba diving or something else new and different that doesn't relate to your prior life. You have to try explicitly to do that. When it's two families coming together, you need something that is unique to the two of you because you want to marry a person, not a group of people. I wasn't marrying a group of five people, and Joan wasn't marrying me and my three daughters; we were interested in marrying each other. How can you even know if that person is right for you if your time together is about making sure kids get fed and take baths, and seeing kid movies all the time? A lot of people who have kids forget what they are interested in because they haven't seen a movie that wasn't a cartoon in five years.

Remarriage and the first year

In looking back, I see the first year of my marriage as a period when some of the inevitable changes happened, especially the changes I had been putting off so I could go along and not make waves. I changed jobs and moved back to Utah, their mom also changed jobs. She got married within a few months of my marriage and moved an hour farther away. This required changes to the custody situation almost immediately. When you have a joint custody situation and then you move too far apart to make that practical, someone has to be primary and someone has to be non-primary. I didn't feel that I had done anything to lose custody, and I didn't see any reason why I should not be the main caregiver, but Mary felt she should be the primary caregiver. There was no way to satisfy both parties.

Ultimately I felt like I could either accept a lesser role or go to court and fight it all the way to the top. Custody laws being what they are and Utah being a conservative state, I realized that I would probably lose. I was unlikely to be given primary custody unless their mom had done something horrifically wrong. I was not happy about it, but I didn't believe I had any options. So, the kids stayed with their mom and I wound up with reduced parent time. I've experimented with different things. I tried the standard weeknight visits where the noncustodial parent gets one week night in the middle of the week, but that required a lot of driving. It was two hours of driving for an hour and a half with me and Joan. The kids didn't have enough time to get comfortable before they had to start leaving again. That didn't work out well and we eventually quit doing it.

Joan and I tried to come up with an arrangement that would work, but to be blunt, I don't think their mother was ever going to be happy. She wanted to be sole custodial parent, so everything that reminded her that she wasn't was met with hostility. Today, for example, the kids are with us significantly more on weekends than at their mom's house. Their church membership is at our house. They go to church with us most Sundays, but there are also a lot of weekday activities where the teens get together, and they do that with their mom's church group in her town. My ex has tried to use that as leverage to get my time with the kids reduced, saying it would be better to spend Sundays with her too. Frankly, if we didn't fight to protect our time with my kids I wouldn't see them for ten minutes a year.

It's been a hard transition. I don't always know how to handle things. For example, handling school events and activities has been hard. If they're going to be in orchestra they ought to talk with me about this; if they're in plays, especially if there are rehearsals on the weekends, they ought to talk with me about that. I ought to know what classes they are in and so forth. But because their mother works in the school district, she has a much closer tie to all those school activities, and she rules them with an iron fist. And so I usually don't hear about those things anymore. It is more frustrating for Joan than for me because she sees me getting left out of things and her protective defenses come out on my behalf. We do that a lot for each other—I've noticed that we're much more aware of our spouse getting what we feel is a raw deal than we are of ourselves.

The first year there was a lot of interaction between the two households, significantly more than now. As that proved to be unhelpful, it declined pretty rapidly. That was the period when I realized this heavy interaction model does not work for me. It was never about things that I cared about; it was always about what I could do for their mother. It's gotten to the point with my ex that I've asked the court to stipulate email contact only between us, and even then only on certain topics. To make that work, I've made a conscious decision to let Mary's house do their thing and we'll do ours. It's a lot less interaction, and maybe I don't know everything that happens anymore, but there's been a lot less conflict.

My relationship with my stepchildren

I met my stepchildren the first time at a buffet. The older two were thirteen and eleven at the time. I didn't know how to handle boys that age. I tried to be "buddy buddy" with them, saying things like "Hey, dude, you want a soda?" I think they were fine with me, but I doubt they were impressed with me. I wanted to be cool, but I was pretty clueless. Luckily for me, our society has defined the role of the father broadly, from someone who is very caring and involved to someone who is almost like a scout leader. It gives men more leeway to figure out where on the spectrum they want to be. I think I took the scout leader approach the first time I met Joan's kids. To their credit, they like me anyway.

My relationship with each of the stepkids has ended up differently, which is not surprising. The oldest one has had the least close relationship with me. He was never comfortable with me as a father figure, but now that he is eighteen, he is looking for more man-to-man advice. The younger ones tended to bond with me sooner because they still needed a father figure. The youngest girl was four when I met her and she has spent significantly more time with me than with her own father. She feels that even though she has another dad, I am the dad she has every day. She has the one that comes every few months and one who is here all the time.

I think one thing that has helped with the second boy is that we found a common interest. He is our only child involved in sports. He decided he wanted to try rugby, which is a sport I could learn alongside of him. We even took at trip to Las Vegas for a tournament. Rugby is something we have used as an "us" thing.

There are parenting things that I am good at. For example, I am the one who is constantly nagging the kids to do their homework. When the kids do their homework, I feel good about that. I'm able to say that this is a way I have contributed to these children's lives. When I see the things that my stepkids are getting from me, the things I have tried to instill in them, I feel rewarded.

When it comes to discipline, we have found that it is much easier to discipline our own kids than the stepkids. There's a different dynamic with stepchildren because, unlike your own children, you have not raised them from infancy. This leads to misinterpretations. Early on, Joan might say, "Karen's been glaring at me all day." I'd look at Karen and think, "Really? I'm not seeing that." Joan didn't have that history with Karen to know she's not angry. Because you don't have that context of years and years, you can get different signals from the same things. And because you are still new to each other, you can each feel insecure. That doesn't work well when it comes time to discipline a child.

Joan's relationship with my daughters

Joan has put a lot of effort into being a mother to my kids, to the point of stepping up when their mom isn't providing the basic emotional support they need. She has been hurt many times because my kids have had loyalty issues with their mom. The closer they get to Joan, the harder their mother makes it for them. She uses guilt, implying that if they like Joan they're being disloyal to her. Sometimes she spends the long drive back to their house criticizing anything good that happened while they were here. She has a very impressive bag of tricks to try and keep them from getting too close to Joan as a mother. With that much pressure, the stepparent relationship can really be fragile.

When stepkids are bratty, indifferent, or unkind, it has a much bigger impact on a stepmom than when her biological kids act that way. Are they being snotty because they are teenagers or because they have a loyalty thing to their mom? When something goes bad, as it inevitably does in every relationship, all those old feelings are still there on the edge waiting for an opportunity to show themselves again. Is this a loyalty thing? Are they lashing out at you because the other parent wants them to? Or are they just being a bratty teenager? Joan and I tell all our kids, "You don't get the luxury of being indifferent. If you are choosing to be indifferent you are choosing to be mean." We tell them they need to think about the impact they are having on the stepparent, and they need to tell their stepparent how they are feeling.

The world needs stepmoms. My kids wouldn't be anywhere near as healthy if Joan didn't keep trying to be there for them, even when it's hard. I think kids need someone who is willing to make that extra effort. I have seen improvement in our family as a group and in each kid individually. Part of that is getting more comfortable with each other and the roles we have in our family unit, and part of it is feeling less at risk. The reservoir of goodwill is getting deeper everyday with the stepkids because we are having more good experiences with them that we can draw from when things are difficult.

My relationships with the other dads

Meeting Joan's second husband, Fred, was horrifically

awkward. He was still single and hadn't gotten a new family of his own, so it was the fifth-wheel effect. I've actually spoken to him now, but we didn't speak the first time or probably the first four or five times. It was like we were passing each other in a room and not acknowledging each other. I wasn't threatened by him in any way, but I thought he was threatened by me, and so there was this weird power dynamic that made it awkward and uncomfortable. It's still very distant. He comes into town for a weekend once every few months to see Jared and Lilly.

Meeting the other ex-husband, Mike, was not too bad at all. Not all sunshine and roses, but it certainly wasn't awkward in the same way. He is married and has stepkids, and he and his wife have kids of their own as well. Their situation is similar to ours. It's like two families meeting each other, not a guy meeting his ex-wife's family. Also, Joan and Mike were divorced so long ago that they have settled into a comfortable relationship. Whatever anger they had burned out long ago. He has Thomas and Bob most summers.

I don't have any relationship with Mary's husband at all. He's got a personality that I wouldn't get along with even without the ex-wife baggage. We had more interaction early on but it tended to disintegrate into hostility pretty rapidly. It started as "Let's bring in mom's new husband as a middle man." But he's certainly not going to be a neutral middle man, and so it really wasn't an effective strategy. Of course, he is very much on their mom's side. He's bowed out of any interaction with me or our family. I'm not a fan of his.

Joan's relationship with Mary, my ex-wife

The first meeting between Joan and Mary was incidental and awkward. I handled it poorly, so I am embarrassed to even tell the story. Joan was at my apartment and my ex came to drop off the girls. Joan went into the bedroom with the girls to change their clothes, and I started talking with my ex. We talked about getting ready to move and looking at apartments, and when Joan came back in, much to my shame, I ignored her and continued talking with my ex. Feeling like a fifth wheel, she stood there thinking, "Why am I even here?" I realized that I was doing this all wrong. I shifted gears and started paying attention to Joan, but Mary stayed for another twenty minutes. She wanted to be part of the scene: me, Joan, the girls and the ex, all mixed together. She really didn't want me to have a family relationship that didn't include her. I probably should have made her leave sooner. The whole interaction was really awkward. In hindsight it was a sign of things to come.

Mary was immensely threatened by Joan. She wanted her to be either her co-mother or her slave. There was never any option for Joan to be independent. The relationship between Joan and my ex-wife is a power struggle where my ex feels threatened in her relationship with her children and feels that someone is trying to displace her. It seems like introducing a new parent can bring up some of those instinctive, protect-the-offspring reactions from women more than from men. I guess maybe men tend to feel protective of the group while women tend to feel protective of the individual.

Maybe we need to recognize that the relationship between the mother and the stepmother is always going to have some risk associated with it. I'm not saying it will never be good, I'm just saying that the ones that are good have figured out how to negotiate that risk and make it so that both women feel that they have a stable, unthreatened position. Honestly, the easiest way for that to happen is to cut one person off completely. And you see that. I would bet that cutting one person out is a lot more common than what I would think of as real "co-parenting." You see stepmoms who aren't allowed to do anything for their stepkids, or you see stepmoms who do well because the mom is out of the picture. Those two extremes are a lot easier than trying to get along with each other. But what do you do when you have a situation that is more normal, where there is some involvement from both, where both want to be there for the kids and make them happy? But there is just this feeling of "That's my job, not your job," with a lot of moms trying to protect their territory. The fact is that most stepmoms feel unappreciated.

My kids were very drawn to Joan. Whatever conflict there is between Joan and my children comes from the sense of loyalty they have to their mother, trying to satisfy everyone, and feeling guilty for having strong feelings for Joan that they have been told they should have only for their mother. They feel stress and tension because they think, "People aren't okay with me liking both of them." I speak from direct personal experience. It does not matter how much the adult says they're okay with it. If they are not, kids can tell. You could have asked my ex-wife a thousand times, "Are you okay with Joan fulfilling this role?" She would say, "Yes, absolutely," because she knows that is what she is supposed to say. But she is not okay with it and we can all feel it, and her children can feel it. It affects how her children, my children, interact with Joan.

I have made a shift in thinking over the last couple of years, away from the guy-centric solve-the-problem approach to trying to have an approach that looks at my relationships. What I've noticed is that when we as stepparents feel safe and affirmed, only then do we feel the freedom to focus on solving problems. Rather than having to drag everyone into the middle, if we can make people feel safe in their relationships, they will come to the middle on their own. If a stepparent feels like they don't have the support of their spouse, it's much harder for them. If you can put your spouse first, they are then secure enough that they are able to help you meet the children's needs. On the other hand, if you neglect your relationship with your spouse to focus on the kids, it actually backfires because you have to do all the work alone. If we can feel comfortable and stable as parents and as a couple, then the two of us can work together and find a solution to the problem with the kid.

This approach doesn't come naturally to me and it doesn't always feel obvious, but it works. Joan needs to feel validated as a parent first, and then I can worry about the kids second. The two of us, once she feels safe and supported, can say, "Okay, so I think that is more than what that kid can handle. Can we do something else?" First, step away from solving the problem. Be loyal to your wife. Place that foundation underneath her so you can work together.

Reflections

One thing that is true, whether it should be or not, is that because the bar is set so much lower for stepdads, success is a lot easier to achieve. Because there is more range for success for a stepfather than a stepmother, I would think the appropriate role for a stepdad is to be the flexible one.

Be willing to adapt, be the one who is adjusting to the situation and trying to fit into the role that works best. Most of the other people in our stepfamily dynamic are in a role they are locked into. The kids are locked into this: "I'm biologically and emotionally attached to my mom. I have a stepmom who is trying to reach out to me and be emotionally there for me, and I am conflicted." They are just stuck. The stepmom sometimes feels stuck too, thinking, "What is my role? I have to be more than a babysitter, but I can never be as good as a mom." In most situations, the stepdad is the only person who has some flexibility. Take advantage of that. Use the flexibility to help heal some of the wounds and negotiate some of the rocky passages.

The hardest thing for me as a parent is finding a way to deal with problems that feels fair and right. If one of my kids does something wrong and one of my stepkids does the exact same thing, what should I do? I can't say, "This is your kid, you deal with it." If I ground a kid for a week, for some that affects them for seven days, and for others it's only two. Or sometimes my kids might leave a mess and I don't see it till after they leave for their mother's house. Now what? I won't see them for a week. Do I harbor resentment till they get back or blow it off? Neither option feels right to me. This goes for positive things they do as well. If a kid gets a day of being rewarded, for my stepkids that's just one day, but for one of my kids that might be their whole time with the family for two weeks. Equal treatment is a myth. Your goal should be that all the kids feel equally valued and equally loved.

This isn't easy. For example, when I'm talking with the kids, I often use a nickname. One day I said to my stepdaughter, "How are you doing, Shorty?" My daughter looked at me surprised with a hurt look in her eyes and said, *"I'm* Shorty." I hadn't realized that she thought that was a special name—it was just something I called the little kids. I said, "I'm sorry, you're Shorty too, but I didn't think that was a nickname just for you, and I'm not going to stop calling your stepsister that either." But I'm thinking, "Great, now what? I'm going to have to write down every interaction with seven different kids just to keep track of who thinks they own what nickname." That was when I became aware that there was some potential rivalry that I wasn't seeing. The way I've tried to handle this is that my stepkids have a right to have me as a dad as much as my own kids do. Honestly I don't know if that works well. Joan said something that has stuck with me. "Would you rather be right or would you rather be happy?" Focus on what you need to do to be happy and to have a good experience. Sometimes you have to let go of a need for justice. Ingrained in our nature is to want things to be fair and right, and things are just not going to happen that way. It's not always easy.

Joan's Story

What does family mean to you?

My idea of family has changed since I've had the blended family experience. When I was young, I would have said that family is blood. Now I think that family are the people that care about you, support you, and love you unconditionally. Even when you make mistakes, they always love you and want you to be happy. They give you the benefit of the doubt whenever conflicts arrive or there are hard things to face. You can have problems and issues, but there is no doubt that at the end of the day, you really love each other.

Growing up

My mother was fifteen when she had me, and then shortly after she had my brother. Our dad ran out on her when I was about two. I had no contact with him until I was an adult. At the age of seventeen, as a single mom with two kids, my mother moved to Utah and met my stepdad. My mom and stepdad had three more kids, and the five of us were raised as one family. We were really tight. I never thought of my three sisters as half siblings. We were active in the LDS church, but because our family was such a mess, I never felt I fit in with the culture, although I believed in the religion very much.

My stepdad was an angry, violent man. He beat the living tar out of me from the time I was three until I was sixteen. Sometimes when he was angry, I would deliberately instigate a fight with him, because then he would just get mad at me and leave the others alone. I knew his behavior was wrong. I remember looking at my mom from the time I was small and thinking, "Get your shit together." She was always sick or sad. I knew my sisters needed something better. I wanted them to have happy days and good experiences. I was scared to talk to anyone about what was going on in the house. My mother would say that if I told people what was going on, the child protective services would come and put us in foster care and my sisters would be molested. I believed that. I thought it was my job to keep our family intact and my sisters safe. I always knew it was wrong the way things were, and I knew that if I had kids, things would be different. I would make my home happy, a place to feel good, because it didn't feel good to grow up in my home.

Luckily, I had a good friend. One night after spending

the night at my house, she told me, "Your mom is crazy." It was the first time I didn't feel responsible for my mother's behavior. From then on I practically lived at my friend's house. Her family had their problems, but they loved each other, and I felt safe there. I learned how a home could feel. You could be a kid there. You could make mistakes and it was fine. I named my youngest daughter after that friend.

When I turned eighteen, I left home and moved in with my boyfriend. I stayed with him for about a year. Soon after I moved out, my mom divorced my stepdad, married someone else, divorced him and married someone else, and now they are separated. Most of her life has been about trying to keep a man, yet she doesn't stay married. As I look back I can see that I learned early on to cut and run when a relationship faced challenges, and it has been something I have struggled with my entire adult life. Now I know that once you have kids you have to choose something better. I don't think my mother ever understood that.

Mike, husband one

After breaking up with my boyfriend, I met my first husband, Mike. He was eight years older than I was, but kind of in the same place in life, despite his age. He grew up in a Mormon family, one of seven kids. Neither of us had any direction. We were figuring it out as we went along. When I got pregnant I decided to marry him. I thought, "I'll try and make it work." But it was never a good relationship. We fought like cats and dogs.

Mike got a job doing grounds keeping, and I was a stay-at-home mom. In our church culture, women are heavily encouraged to stay at home with their kids. I liked taking care of my kids. We were married for four years and had two boys, Thomas and Bob.

Before our first child, Thomas, turned a year old, we separated because the marriage was horrible. I went to live with my family but then I thought, "This is too hard. I'd rather try and figure it out with Mike." I went back, got pregnant again and within a year realized that nothing was harder than living with someone you hate. Everything was a fight; everything was an issue. Shortly after, I asked for a divorce.

Even though we had divorced, we continued to fight. We didn't settle child support for almost a year. Then one day for whatever reason, Mike had a change of heart. I think he just kind of forgave me for leaving, and we started working together. The fighting stopped, and we have never fought since. I was given full custody of Thomas and Bob. He saw them every other weekend and every other holiday, but if he had time off, I let him see the kids. I thought, "I have the privilege of living with the kids and taking care of them. He wouldn't mind trading places with me." So every time he wanted to see the kids, I let him. I had the luxury of having them every day. I needed to make sure he knew he was still their parent as well. So I let the kids see him more often than the state guidelines permitted.

I think people underestimate how much it hurts to go from being a parent who sees their child every day to having to follow some court mandated schedule and get permission from an ex just to see their child. Nobody has a baby and thinks, "I am going to be the best parent every other weekend." You love your kids 24/7 and getting divorced with a custody schedule does not change the fact that you want to be with them every day; it's just the other parent you don't want to be around.

Seven years after our divorce, Mike remarried. Her name was Sharon, and she had three kids already. They have had two more together. Mike thought Sharon and I should meet before the wedding and see if I approved of her being in the boys' lives. But he didn't need my permission. Even if she had been a shrew, it wasn't my choice. It was his choice. I met her a week before the wedding, and I asked her how I could help. She asked if I could drive the boys to the wedding. Done. Everything was pretty seamless.

Sharon and I got along very well. She is very different from me, but she is the salt of the earth, a great woman. We are friendly but not friends. It is comfortable, relaxed, and easy. But I will admit that the first time Bob came home and he referred to her as *Mom*, all the hair on the back of my neck stood up. Then I thought, "Well, my kids call my husband Dad. This is just a title. This takes nothing from me. Call her whatever name you want as long as it's nice." The kids didn't get to choose when their parents got divorced, and they didn't get to choose when their parents got remarried or when or if they got a stepfamily. They could choose the relationship they had with the stepparent, as long as it was one that worked. For us it worked. Bob continued to call Sharon, Mom. He thought the name was respectful. Thomas, on the other hand, told her, "You are not my mom; you are Sharon." Thomas was respectful about it, but he was not comfortable calling her Mom.

Our households are different. Thomas didn't like to go to his dad's because his dad didn't have a computer system, and they had more rules than we did. Mike and Sharon are much more religious and stricter than we are. I am a pretty permissive parent and they are not. They never miss church and they fast on Sundays. Thomas and his dad would get into fights over theology and politics, and Thomas would get mad and run away. It was complicated and hard. His dad wanted to work it through, but Thomas kept pushing for more say in his schedule. It became a very rough situation and was causing a lot of contention in their home. My position was that I would follow the court order and insist on the visits, but I could not physically force Thomas to visit his dad or keep him from running away. I needed them to find something that worked. Finally Mike said that if Thomas didn't want to come to their home, they wouldn't make him. I know that was hard for Mike and Sharon, and I continued to remind Thomas that he needed to make the effort and try harder to find common ground.

While I supported Thomas, I wanted him to have a good relationship with his other family, and I wanted him to learn that it wasn't okay to run away from his problems. War and submission are the two extremes in relationships, and I knew it was important for Thomas to find a comfortable place in between. He needed some space in order to appreciate the things he had at his dad's house, and their relationship has been improving over time.

Fred, husband two

Shortly after my divorce from Mike, I met Fred. He seemed perfect. Everything was right. He had graduated from Brigham Young University, he was a returned missionary, he had a job, and he was a grown-up. He was also nine years older then I was. Although he was older, we were in the same place and knew where we wanted our lives to go. Fred and I got married and had two kids together, Jared and Lilly. We were married for eight years. He was even more permissive than I was as a parent. He has a religious background in Mormonism and Scientology, and one of his beliefs is "Don't change who that person is going to be. Let them be the master of their destiny." He never said no to anything ever, ever, ever. Whatever anyone said, he would say, "Yes, that's a great idea." At the time I first met him, I felt I had had so much judgment and rejection in my last marriage, that a marriage to a person who never said no would be bliss. I didn't realize that if he was going to say yes to me and to the kids, that he would also say yes to everyone and everything that came his way. It was an impossible way to live, and the children needed an actual parent, not just smiling wall art.

It was a loveless marriage. We got along, but there wasn't any connection. I was very lonely and depressed. I had a marriage with no emotions. We decided to separate. I moved to Utah, and he took a job in New Jersey to give us space to work out our marriage. During that time, Fred decided to come clean and one day on the phone, he told me that he had been having gay affairs for the past two years. I filed for divorce the next day. I got this insane divorce settlement. Utah can be very mother-friendly and it was to me. I got the house and a huge alimony. Fred told me that he wanted me to be able to stay home with the kids, so he paid twice the child support that the state recommended so I didn't have to work.

Both of my ex-husbands loved their kids more than they hated me. Fred especially knew that his behavior had caused the breakup of our marriage and family, and he wanted to do what he could so that the kids did not pay a high price. He knew that if I had to rejoin the workforce at that time, it would be too much of a change for the kids. He didn't want to have the guilt of forcing that on us just because he had cheated. I agreed and was able to continue to stay at home with the kids after our divorce. Thomas was devastated by the divorce. He wasn't super close to Fred, but he was thirteen when we divorced, starting to see himself as a man and needing a role model. He was already pissed off at his biological father who he thought was a closed-minded, conservative republican, Glenn Beck stereotype. Now the other male in his life was going in the complete opposite direction. He got really depressed. I worried a lot about him. Bob, on the other hand, rolls with the punches. He took the divorce in stride and did really well. Jared and Lily stayed the same. Fred wasn't that involved with them when we were married. He's never going to be a very involved parent; however, he does visit the kids regularly. He maintains a good relationship with all of the kids, just at an arm's length. Parenthood is a messy experience for him, and he has an aversion to such things.

Harry, husband three

When I divorced Fred my plan was to take care of my kids and do my own thing. I also knew that I needed to stop this crap about having stupid, bad relationships, and making choices that I thought were getting me out of an emergency but then lasted for years and years. I thought I could figure myself out. I knew I had the tools. I just needed a break, so I thought, "I'm just going to be a mom."

But I would sometimes get bored and lonely, so I went online to church-based dating sites to give myself a social outlet. I love to go to movies, and I like dinners, but I wasn't looking to re-couple. But at the same time I didn't want to stay at home all day and be a spinster either. So one night when I was bored and irritated with a guy I'd been dating, I sent a message to every guy on the "online now" list who was local and 6 foot 4 or over. I'm tall; I like tall guys. Harry just happened to be one of them. He responded. We went on a date and he told me that he knew the minute he saw me that I was the one. It took me longer to know he was my soul mate; I didn't know until the next day.

We dated for about four months, and then Harry got a job transfer to Chicago. The beauty of his being transferred was that I could visit him on weekends. That was our time. We got to be a couple and have long talks. That was our foundation. Even though we both had kids (he had three daughters), we became "us" in Chicago. Now, when we are going in a hundred different directions with all of these kids, we look back at that time and think, "It can be like that again when all the kids move out." We know that we are a happy couple and that is what bonds us together; we are not just together for the kids. We love the kids, but we needed to be secure in the one-on-one relationship as well. Neither of us had that in the past with our prior spouses. We still go to Chicago every year or so just to remember that this is where we figured out that we should be together, and every other month we do a weekend away, just the two of us. Now that the kids are older, we can go out and have regular date nights together.

Harry's ex-wife, Mary

While we were dating, Harry told me a little bit about his ex-wife. He said "I don't want to rock the boat because she will go crazy on the kids. You guys will be friends." I told him that I pick my own friends, thank you; it would depend on me and her. He said, "I promised her that whoever I picked would be her friend." I could tell he was afraid. He had a lot of anxiety.

When Mary and I met, I could understand why. She kind of blew in the door. No one introduced me. She was dressed like a gypsy with lots of scarves, bangle earrings, and hair things. She had so many accessories that I thought she was wearing her whole closet. She gave Harry a hug, took him by the arm and led him into the living room. I'm thinking, "Is this happening?" I took Harry's kids into their bedroom so they could change out of their church clothes. When I went back into the living room, she had her arm around his shoulder. She looked over at me and gave me that "cat-with-the-bird-in-its-mouth smile." I'm thinking, "This is not right."

I got my purse and headed for the door. Harry asked, "Where are you going?" I said, "I gotta go home. This is weird. I didn't come here to watch you and Mary have some weird, crazy divorced-people date." He was uncomfortable and didn't want me to leave, but he didn't know what to do. Mary wanted to be there, with us, and he was afraid to tell her "no." I told him he needed to figure his stuff out and that I had to go. He didn't want that, but he did not know how to navigate the situation. He just started to ignore Mary, and she eventually got angry and left in a huff. Within the hour the calls started coming. She wanted to be an active part of our relationship: he needed to answer to her, run things by her and make sure I understood that I *had* to be her friend. It was the weirdest thing I had ever seen. Having been in her shoes, I could not understand her possessive behavior.

At first, I didn't trust Harry with his ex. I thought that whenever he was alone with her they would talk about the good old days. I didn't trust that he wasn't interested in her, because I could see how interested in him she was. I felt the need to be part of everything. If she emailed something, I had to see it. I didn't trust that he had moved on, because it was clear that she felt they had a relationship that was very different from what he said they had. I wish I had had more self confidence and that I could have said, "If there is something that matters, then we can talk about it. Other than that, you handle it. Don't tell me about it." But I had such a hard time trusting him. I know a lot of women who feel this way. Now I ignore a lot, especially if it's high conflict. And now Harry is more secure in his role as a father and is no longer as easily manipulated by Mary. He knows who he is as a parent and no longer believes he needs her permission to be a parent.

For a short time, I had issues around the fact that Harry had had children with her and not with me. It came from a place of insecurity. I know it sounds petty, but it is how I felt. It wasn't that I wanted more kids, but I wanted Harry and me to share that special thing. I wanted him to feel our baby kicking inside my belly. I wanted to go to the doctor with him, to pick out names—the whole baby dream. In my head there was magic when they had their children. I trumped that up to a crazy level. Then I met a woman at church who was talking about her grandkids and how she loved being with them. I realized that if I had a baby now I wouldn't have the time and energy to be a good grandma when my kids had children. I realized what I wanted was to feel bonded with Harry, what I wanted was to have special things with him. I didn't want a baby. His having a baby with Mary took nothing from me or our relationship, and it didn't make his marriage to her magic. Then I felt at peace. I never really considered having a baby with Harry again. I could feel complete in my role as a wife and mother.

I felt that Mary was a cuckoo mom and that I could help the girls. She hadn't taught them even basic skills. I taught them how to fix their hair, how to navigate social situations, what to do when they got their period. The girls asked me about all of these things, and I felt they were things a mother should teach a daughter, but Mary just refused. When I'd try and talk to her to see if she would have these conversations with her daughters, she'd laugh and tell me that wasn't important to her. The girls needed a mother, and Mary was primarily interested in being their peer and getting credit for things. It seemed to me that her primary goal was to be cool to her kids, cooler than their stepmom, that's for sure. I let her be the cool one; I let her get away with treating me like an employee.

Harry's girls wanted to call me Mom before we were even engaged. I thought this wasn't healthy. They were very needy. Looking back, I think Harry expected me to come and save everyone, and I thought I could, but I was amazed at how fast a word could take the wind out of my sails. Harry didn't set boundaries with his ex-wife, and she wouldn't let go. She saw herself not only as the mother but as Harry's wife. Mary and I have never had a civil or helpful conversation. I think we both tried, but it was always a weird power dynamic.

I tried to co-parent the first year. I tried to find something that worked, but nothing did. She needed to be in control, and I am just not wired that way. To be blunt, you can't co-parent with a person who thinks the "co" means "control." So Harry and I focused on parallel parenting instead. Mary made it clear that she blamed me for everything.

Bringing our families together

In Mormon culture we are family-focused and sometimes we move fast on these things. Harry and I were just so compatible and worked so well together. I knew he was the right person, so after six months of dating, we got married. My oldest son, Thomas, who was twelve at the time, wasn't thrilled. I think he thought: "Here we go again." The others cheered.

We had a pretty small wedding. One of the movies we loved was *Joe Versus the Volcano*. That's been our theme in life. We'll jump into the volcano and no matter what happens we'll work it out. We had the wedding in Harry's brother's backyard. We decorated with orange soda cans, and fake tiki dolls. I was barefoot. His brother has a creek in his backyard, and the kids all jumped into the water. It was perfect for us—playful and easy going. Thomas had a great time. Harry rolled up his pants, jumped right in the water, and started dunking him. Later Thomas told me, "Harry will be a big brother to me. Not my dad, but a big brother." A big brother was just fine. I feel very strongly that while a stepchild does not get to choose whether they have a stepparent, they do get to choose what type of relationship they will have, as long as it is respectful.

We moved into a house that, even though it needed work, had enough square footage that everyone had their own space, and everyone could feel like they were home. We put our bedroom on the main floor with all the kids' bedrooms upstairs. This way we could have some sort of alone time in the evening. The kids were part of all the decisions. We made sure that Harry's girls had their place at our house. What we wanted were nine happy people in the house. It was our home; everyone was a vital part of our household.

At first, we had a lot of family meetings. We wanted to find solutions that actually worked for the individuals in our home. It didn't matter if we did everything "right," if it didn't actually work. We asked the kids: What will work? What do you want? We talked openly. We followed our gut; we prayed. We tried to figure out what worked and what felt right instead of what people tell you is right. I knew if there were things we didn't know, I had a partner who wanted to find the right answers. We weren't going to say, "This is how we are going to parent and we are sticking with that." I knew we could change directions if things weren't working. I took things one day at a time. I figured that we would roll with the punches and figure it out. A stepfamily is a fluid thing.

We developed ground rules about discipline. Ultimately the biological parent is the disciplinarian. If the kids break rules and need a consequence, you need to tell the biological parent. There is absolutely no corporal punishment under any circumstances to any child. You can say, "Knock it off; stop it; you have to do this chore now." But if it is a serious or sensitive issue, the biological parent needs to take the lead. Sometimes, it is easier if you think of your stepchildren as nieces and nephews. They are family and you love them, but there are boundaries when it comes to disciplining the children of your sibling. You guide and help, but if a niece or nephew is in need of a time-out, you have the actual parent do it. There are lines you would never cross. If there is a problem, Harry and I talk about it, but the biological parent decides what's right and makes the decisions. When Harry and I have strongly disagreed on how to handle a kid situation, we both have had to step back and just go with what the child's bio-parent feels is right. Sometimes this requires a lot of communication, and feelings get bruised, but we each have a subtle but greater role as a bio-parent and that needs to be respected. There are times we both just bite our tongues and say, "Okay, it's your kid." We still support each other, even if we don't agree on a specific course of action.

When we first got together, we told the kids they could call us what they wanted. Thomas chose to call Harry by his first name. Bob called him Dad; my other two called him Dad as well. The girls called me Mom. That worked for the first year. I had told the girls, "Don't call me something that your mom won't be okay with." First, Mary had been fine with them choosing to call me Mom, but a year later, out of the blue, she screamed at the girls, "Don't call her Mom." The girls were really hurt. One weekend they didn't know what to call me so they didn't use any name. We had a family meeting. I told them to call me Joan or Mom, but not to call me "you there." They decided to call me Mom, but it's not really about what they call me. It's whatever makes them comfortable. It's complicated. I am the mother of the house, and yet I am only the biological mother of some of the kids. I wish that the girls felt as comfortable to choose as my bio-kids do. They want to call me Mom, but they also feel guilty for doing so. I have asked them to just give me another nickname, but they have not wanted to do that.

I don't invest in Harry's girls as much as when we first got married. There is a barrier between us. Do I sit and braid Charity's hair and talk with her about the woman she's turning into? No. Do I do that with Maggie? Sometimes, sure. She's littler; she's closer. She was younger when we got married. She looks for that nurturing. Charity is aware that anytime she gets close to me she gets in trouble with her mom. I don't want her to get in trouble. I'm just her stepmom. Kids are going to feel loyalty to the other parent; they are going to be pulled. You can expect that. If there is a big event coming up like a church event or graduation, kids are going to get weird. If they have to pick a relationship they can withdraw from, pick me. I don't have the same needs as their bio-parents. My identity is not rolled up in them the way it is for a bio-parent. I don't want to be the source of their pain. It's hard enough they have a stepmom. I don't want to be another person who sucks their soul out because I have needs they have to meet. I want to be a stable force and an example. When the kids have conflicts I want to be there for them.

Harry and I do everything we can to make our home a happy home, a peaceful home. Our faith helps a lot. Harry has always been a very hands-on, involved father and stepfather. Jared and Lilly completely see him as a dad. They believe they have two dads. They are aware that their biological dad is their real dad, but they lean on Harry and see him as any child would see a real father. Harry and Bob do sports together. They're pretty close. Harry has become like an older brother to Thomas. Not super close. There is harmony in the house. They know they can count on Harry, and my ex-husbands do not feel that they are getting their toes stepped on. They don't see him as a threat who is trying to steal their children, as is often the case with bio-mothers and stepmoms.

I think society is more forgiving of a man who steps in and fills a parenting role. It's usually looked at as normal and good. When a woman comes into the picture, nothing she does is right and every move she makes is suspect. She has no right coming in and being a mother, whereas it is deemed as natural for a man to do that very same thing. Mary's husband certainly gets no flack when he takes an aggressive parenting role with the girls; however, if I take them to get their hair trimmed, Mary thinks I need to learn my place.

Reflections

It's very hard to be a stepmom. It's hard to be a mom, but being a stepmom has been so much harder than I ever thought. You get so many conflicting messages from society and from the current psychological thinking. I don't think it's realistic that you can love your stepkids like your own kids. I think it's something that we tell ourselves that we should do, but I don't think it's realistic. You look at your kids and you would die for your kids. You look at your stepkids and you think, "If I die for my stepkids, my kids won't have a mother."

Your stepchild might stab you in the back, and you have to let it go. You have to expect it and sometimes you have to let them hurt you. You disagree with it, you cry and you vent to your husband that the kids are being shits, and then you get up the next day, put their laundry away, and you tell them they look nice today. Same thing you do with your bio-kids, I guess. You do the best you can. I tell my boys to treat their stepmom as though she were gold. She has never been abusive or done anything outside of being a different type of mother than I am. She has different needs and values, but she has the right to feel as though her role is important. I don't care what she does; she's putting up with those kids and hasn't killed them yet. I may think the boys are perfect children, but I know they bring with them baggage that is heavy to deal with. I thank her so much for not giving up on kids who look and act like her husband's ex-wife much of the time.

One of the biggest things that helped me was an online support group. When things got really bad and Harry was getting dragged into court or mediation about every three months, I got to the point where I was ticked off so much that I joined a group called "I hate my stepkids." I vented at how irritated I was, and we laughed and made horrible jokes. It's okay not to be the Brady Bunch or the Von Trapp family. It was a safe place to bring out my petty issues with Mary and the anger I was having while I smiled through the tears here at home. The group would also say, "You have a good husband; let's help you deal with the crap." They helped me focus on making sure my home and my marriage were strong and reminded me that the rest of the chaos was just temporary. Kids grow and change and the relationships all change over time as well. I needed to hang on, and if I felt like I was going to break down and run for the hills, I could go to them first, dump it all out and then they would help me make the better choice. I could lay my burdens down and it was okay for me not to be perfect. It was okay to talk about my insecurities, stress, and how Mary looked when she picked up the kids.

Having an ongoing support group maybe saved my marriage. I learned that a stepmom is absolutely first and foremost a partner with her husband. She's on his side, and if he is doing things she feels are wrong, they work it out, not in front of the kids or on the kids. They need to figure themselves out as a couple first. If the marriage is strong, the family becomes strong. If Harry and I can handle hard things as a couple, we can lead our whole family through any hard times in the future. He and I needed to find what worked for us as a couple and never let the stress of blending families take away the love and connection we initially found with each other.

Today, most days are great, but sometimes I wonder. Do I know these people? How am I in this situation? A stepfamily takes so much. There are only so many hours in a day and so many dollars to spend. My kids are aware that blending our families has taken a great deal of energy, time, and money. I keep a family blog so that we can remember that for the most part we are really happy. I want my kids to know, all seven of them, that I chose this life with them, with Harry. I want them to know that in spite of the struggles, we have a good life, and we are blessed and lucky to have found each other. For the most part, we really like each other.

John's Story

John, himself a stepchild, is married with one stepson, Gabe, who was seven when his mother Liz and John married. They have two children together, Christine and Jeremy.

What does family mean to you?
I have two definitions of family. The first is where you are related to each other in a genetic or legal sense like your parents, aunts, uncles and grandparents. And then there is the family you create, the people you surround yourself with, the people you love and care about. They might not be related to you in the legal sense.

Growing up
My parents divorced when I was not yet one and my father quickly became involved with and then married another woman who had a son, my stepbrother. My parents were among the earlier ones in our community that got divorced, and by junior high most of the parents were divorced. My mom stayed in Brooklyn with me and my older brother, Luke, and my dad moved to Albany to live with my stepmother and stepbrother. Having Luke was great. He was four years older, so he was able to guide and protect me along that process. Because my parents lived so far apart, we traveled a lot early on.

My mom had expectations about what it meant to be a family, which our new model didn't fit, causing her problems. It didn't cause me problems because my family was what I had; it was all I knew. I did not have the expectation that you have to have a nuclear family. Your family is what it is. A child doesn't know that it's supposed to be different. My mom wanted to have a loving family with a mom and dad where the mom didn't work and raised the kids. That's not how it turned out, and that was painful for her. I saw how that upset her, and then I became upset too. She was constantly comparing what she was able to provide with what my dad could provide. I would tell her, "I don't care that my dad is taking us to Florida and you are taking us to Coney Island. I'll have fun with my family at both places. I have you. And it's great. I don't want something different from what I have."

I learned later in life that my experience growing up in two families was not unlike a bicultural experience. I came to that realization doing anti-oppression work. I heard people talk about their experiences in bicultural or multiethnic families where they had to integrate distinct cultural experiences. In Albany I had a more traditional nuclear family with two parents who were well off, and in Brooklyn I had a single mother who struggled financially. There were different rules in the houses, different ways the families interacted, and different ways they disciplined. There were also significant differences between the two areas: the people, the environment, and the attitudes.

All three of my parents have wonderful things to offer that I have tried to emulate. On the other hand, they all did some things poorly, which I've tried not to do. I have created my own set of choices. I believe that all things being equal, we are generally going to parrot our parents, either by emulating something that worked or doing the opposite of something that didn't. In that way I like to think that we build upon the previous generation and over time strive to create a better family and world. That's the ideal.

I don't believe that divorce is inherently a bad idea. I think there are families who stay together that are much more traumatic than families that get divorced. If I were to get a divorce, I would do my best to do it in such a way as not to make an enemy of my partner or have my children experience trauma. It's possible. I know stepfamilies where the parents, whatever negative energy they have with each other, are able to keep the conflict between each other. They can share social space, or better yet, love each other and be in each other's lives in a healthy way.

Meeting Liz and Gabe

Growing up I thought I would get married and have kids because that is what you were supposed to do. However, by my mid-twenties I had given up on the need to have kids, and then I met Liz. I met her through work. I think what is more significant is *when* I met her. I was going through a transformation, becoming more of an adult. I had cleaned myself up and bought a new car. I knew she had a kid but that didn't give me pause. She definitely wanted more kids, and though I had moved away from needing kids, I still wanted kids. I had no compunctions about being a stepparent. A lot of people are rightfully scared off, and it's a deal breaker. Not me. Probably this was because I had grown up with a single mom and a stepmom I loved and cared about. I also come from a family that is open-minded, so I try not to limit what I say or do or become. Liz is also a stepchild, which she has mixed feelings about.

Liz and her ex-husband were on again off again for the first five years of Gabe's life, and then Liz was alone with Gabe for about a year. They moved a lot. He didn't have a stable home. I met him when we first started dating, but Liz and I decided not to have me interact with him very much for a few months to make sure we wanted to continue seeing each other. We dated "on the under." It was both of our ideas, but Liz spearheaded it. I didn't want to have a relationship with her and then have it not work out and never see her kid again. That would have caused Gabe a lot more trauma than it would me. I was ready to get married and have kids, but not on the first date. Becoming a parent is a process and for a stepparent it's an accelerated process.

When I got into the picture, Gabe and his dad weren't seeing each other much at all. He became more active in Gabe's life when I got involved with Liz. He began to take him on weekends, which meant that Gabe had to go through a shift between parents. This caused emotional distress for him for a couple of days each time. I remember feeling something similar when I was growing up. Ultimately, his dad, who grew up in Peru, moved to Nebraska and had two more kids with another woman.

Now Gabe doesn't see his father often, maybe two or three times a year, and calls his dad about as much as his dad calls him, which is probably about once a month. I feel bad for Gabe. His dad's intentions are there but his actions are not. Also, he does not contribute financially. We even have to pay for Gabe to visit him. We've dealt with it, but it can be frustrating.

Gabe's dad has a lot of wonderful things about him but a lot of faults too. Gabe idolizes his dad, as well he should, but I think his father is failing to provide the level of connection, support, and guidance that Gabe needs. Now with his dad living in Nebraska, it's hard for that relationship to be all that it needs to be. I think this is a subtle tension in Gabe's and my relationship, but I totally understand and don't fault him for it. I don't want to point out the ways his father is not meeting his needs. But, I'm here; I'm here raising him; I'm here sacrificing for him, working hard to provide for him, spending my time and energy developing a relationship with him and caring for him, but his dad can do no wrong. That's frustrating. In social situations when we are being introduced and someone says, "This is Gabe's dad," he says, "No, he is my stepdad." That is a little bit annoying. But it's important to him and I respect that. Gabe is adamant about not considering me his father, but he does consider me his parent. My experience as a stepchild has given me tools to understand Gabe's relationships with his dad, his mom and me, and to be sensitive to the fact that they can be confusing.

Though Gabe's father was not happy about me at first, I believe he has come to accept me and our relationship is fine now. We can share social space, and I have no ill will toward him. I could sit down and have a beer with him. I sense that he has some anger toward me, perhaps because, from his perspective, I have stolen his family, but I think he also sees that I have been able to give Gabe opportunities he would not have been able to give him. I don't need him to acknowledge that. I appreciate that he doesn't fight us about the choices we have made for Gabe and that he wants to be a good father. Gabe and his father have honest love for each other. This means a lot.

Loving your children and wanting the best for them are the foundation of good parenting. The rest is important too, but love goes a long way.

My role as stepfather

At some level, I was always a guiding figure for Gabe. I am a firm believer in the "it takes a village" mentality. If any of my close friends' children need to be told something, I am happy to tell it to them. All of our combined wisdom is important for children to find their way in the world. So if Gabe was chewing with his mouth open, I would say, "You should chew with your mouth closed." I want to raise my children to have the skills and manners to be successful, a combination of what my parents taught me. I've noticed that I have specific ideas about how people should act toward each other. I have these areas where I am fairly strict and others where I am open and free.

Going from friend to parent was a natural process, but a fairly quick one because Liz and I got married about two years after meeting each other. For the first six months, I didn't have a lot of interaction with Gabe, and then Liz moved around the corner from me and I started to spend a lot of time with them. One time I even took care of him for a few days when Liz went out of town for work. Gabe was open to me. He even called me Dad at the very beginning; then one weekend he came back from his dad's and never called me Dad again, which is fine. He can call me anything he wants as long as it's respectful. I called my stepmom by her first name, but then I called all three of my parents by their first names.

Going into this relationship, I knew that Liz's number-one priority was always going to be Gabe and not necessarily me, but I never felt like an outsider. I have to be careful not to put Liz in a situation where she has to choose between us. I don't want to cause her that stress, and I don't want to be shown that I am second tier. I went in with my eyes wide open.

Now we have two more children, Christine and Jeremy. Gabe loves his siblings and is a great big brother. He considers my parents as grandparents, and he certainly has a good relationship with them. I worry, though, that Gabe will feel left out or that we will treat him differently and therefore unfairly. I want to make him feel as loved and nurtured as everyone else. I don't want there to be a difference, but on some level there is and has to be because Gabe is much older than the other two kids, plus Christine is a girl. There are too many things that are different in addition to his being my stepkid. I am heartened by the fact that as Christine has gotten older, I have access to the same places of frustration and anger with her as I have with Gabe. I can get just as annoyed with either of them.

Discipline issues around Gabe have been the main thing Liz and I fight about. While Liz is more protective and defensive of Gabe, I am a little more demanding. She thinks I am too strict and gruff with him. This is a fair criticism, especially when I don't get enough sleep, which is often. This has been exacerbated significantly by my career change in the last four years. I became a firefighter, which meant that I went to a fire academy which is paramilitary. It has changed how I parent. I don't let a lot of things slide, and I want things to be done in a certain way. I come home exhausted. With two other kids, there is less time to just hang out with Gabe. I think that is a problem. I love my kids but it's hard having three. I can say with utmost confidence that none of them gets as much attention as they want. I cannot imagine raising kids on my own. I have even more respect for my mom who did the bulk of raising me and my brother as a single parent.

The biggest challenge for me is that Liz doesn't always assume that I have Gabe's best interests at heart in the way I do with my other children. I don't know to what level that is true, but I feel like that is a tension. I can't say or do things when I'm annoyed, frustrated, or fed up without her assuming on some level that I'm not coming from a place of a loving parent as much as I am with the other children. There can't be any question about them. They are our kids together. I consider Gabe my son, but a stepchild is different from your own child, and ultimately I don't think there is anything that can change that fact. Don't get me wrong, I love him dearly. He is a wonderful, wonderful kid and I do my darndest to treat him fairly. The last time Liz and I had an argument about Gabe, I just told her, "Look, you've got to give me a little credit that I have his best interests at heart, that I love him, care for him and am trying to do the right thing by him. You can't always assume that everything I say is meant to be mean, because I'm not trying to be mean."

Now Gabe is a pre-teen and he is challenging boundaries. He's having a really hard time struggling with the transition from elementary to middle school, and Liz and I are working together as a team to support him. But he is messing up. He isn't turning in his assignments, and he leaves his lunch box at school. To me the consequence should be that he won't be allowed to play competitive soccer, which is what he wants to do. The tryouts are in two weeks and I'll tell you now, Liz and I will be fighting about it. We only have an hour together after he goes to sleep, and if we spend that time arguing with each other, we're not going to enjoy our time together.

Despite all this, I think Gabe is really just a wonderful, wonderful kid. He says and does things that amaze me all the time. I am just happy to be in his life. I'm happy to know him, and I'm happy at the prospect that we are going to share the rest of our lives together. I hope that he is successful in what he wants to do, and I really want to give him skills to do what he wants to do with his life. I say I have three kids. If people ask their ages, I tell them. Then they might ask, "Why is one a lot older?" I tell them that he is my stepkid. Some people tell me he looks like me. We went to make food baskets during the holidays. When we dropped them off, the pastor said, "That must be your son." I just told him, "Thanks."

Reflections

Before you marry a person with children, be sure you want a stepchild in your life. If you are not sure, I could see how this could be a great strain on a relationship. Even though I was sure about Gabe, there have been moments (not recently thankfully) where I thought if this relationship doesn't work out it's because of our struggles around parenting Gabe. Liz doesn't always accept that I am coming from a place of love and kindness, but I have to be really coming from that place. And when I'm tired or frustrated or in a bad mood, that is hard to do. It takes a special kind of person to be a successful stepparent.

I have learned how important it is to be able to communicate with each other. Ultimately, that is what being in a relationship and being a parent is all about. You need to be able to build trust with each other. Liz has to trust that I have Gabe's best interests at heart, and

I have to trust that she is being objective and fair with him and with me. I would hope that on the whole she appreciates how I operate as a stepdad. I think she does. That's not to say that she doesn't have a critique. On the other hand, I appreciate her as a mom. I think she's a great mom; that's not to say she's perfect. If I were not willing to look at how I could improve the way I act toward Gabe, and if Liz were unwilling to hear me or trust me and think about ways she could be different toward Gabe, we probably would not make it. You must be willing to change and look at your own "shit," as it were.

You're going to make mistakes and you're not always going to act in the noblest way. You've got to forgive yourself for that and just keeping trying. As long as Liz and I are trying our best, that is all we can do. If you love and care for your stepchildren and have a genuine desire to do well by them, in the end, the relationship will work out. Let it evolve. Let them come to you. Every relationship is a dance back and forth. Let that dance happen.

Beth's Story

Beth was married for seven years to Jim and had three sons, Alex, Cory, and Jeff. She divorced and married Carl, a man with one daughter, Abigail, who was six at the time. Her sons were five, six and seven when they married. After seventeen years of marriage, after the children had all left home, they divorced.

What does family mean to you?

Family is extremely important to me. It might stem from my father's Mexican/American background where children and family are everything. My father was born in Texarkana, Texas, but his father, who was born in Mexico, moved the family to Salt Lake City, Utah, to avoid the harsh discrimination against Mexicans in Texas. My grandmother was Caucasian with an English background, but they were forced to send their children to segregated schools, and when one child died, they were not allowed to bury him in the cemetery for whites. Salt Lake City had very few Mexicans. When one of my aunts was born, the local newspaper had an article about "the first Mexican baby born in Salt Lake." My grandfather opened the first Mexican restaurant in the city in the early 1900s.

I never knew my grandparents; all of them had died before I was born. My parents moved around quite a lot, finally settling in Montana. I had one sister, six years older, and all of our growing-up years, we would make an annual summer trip to Salt Lake City where most of my father's brothers and sisters lived. My mother was German and Swedish and came from a Mormon background, where family is also important. She had relatives in and around Salt Lake City, and even though my mother was a "Jack Mormon," a person who is a member of the church but does not follow the Mormon principles, her family always welcomed us. So, to me, family means the people who love you and always stand by you no matter what.

First marriage

I wanted to get married and have kids, but I also wanted a career. I worked in an upscale women's clothing store while I was in high school, and I fantasized about becoming a buyer for a fancy store. But I fell in love with my high school sweetheart, Jim. He was heading off to the US Marines and I was planning to go to Chicago to a merchandising school. At the last minute, I changed my mind. We were married a week after graduating from high school, and I ended up in military housing, Camp Pendleton, in Oceanside, California.

We were married for seven years. We had three sons—Alex, Cory, and Jeff—one for each year Jim was in the military. After his service was over, we moved back to our hometown, but we were still very young, and he was unable to adapt to ordinary married life. All of his old buddies were still single, chasing women and drinking a lot. He joined them, leaving me at home with three babies. It was a tough time. I never knew if he would come home at night and often he didn't. I remember lying in bed thinking about where he was. He loved the boys, but he didn't want to give up the party life. It was very difficult.

After years of misery and two trial separations, I divorced

him. My sons were four, five and six when we finally got divorced. This was when I first realized that he had problems with alcohol. It has been a problem all his life continuing to this day. Alcoholism runs in my own family as well. Heredity plays a role in this addiction, and I believe that's a major reason why my sons have also had problems. Today they seem to have figured out how to control it.

Of course, I got full custody of the boys, but my child support was only $180 a month. My job working part-time at JC Penney's just didn't cut it, and I knew I had to do something more to support us, so I applied for grants and loans to go to college. I had a good high school record—Honor Society and all that stuff—plus I was single with three young children. This meant that I was eligible for a lot of financial help. I distinctly remember wanting to jump in the air and click my heels when I walked out of the college financial aid office. I continued my Penney's job and also worked some weekends at the nursery school where I took the boys. Somehow, I patched together enough money, time, and energy to attend classes full-time. I went into the field of education, thinking that teaching was the perfect job for a single mother. I graduated in a little over three years and went on to teach English for twenty-four years at middle school, high school, and community college levels.

Almost as soon as I remarried, Jim quit paying child support. The child support issue haunts me today. I let Jim stop paying without taking him to court. I remember thinking, "I don't need you. I can support my kids without you." What a fool I was. I should have forced him to pay the money and then put it in the bank to use later for the boys' college educations or whatever. I still allowed him to see the boys whenever he wanted to spend time with them. This might have been a mistake as well. But I didn't want them to hate their dad, and I thought that he had some rights to see his kids. He popped in and out of their lives, mostly out. I remember well one time when he had promised to come see them. They stayed at the window all day waiting for him and he never came. I do think he loves his kids. He's just never been dependable.

The boys realized that they weren't high on their father's list of priorities. Sometimes he would take them for a weekend and once or twice he took them to Montana on vacation. I found out later that on one of these trips he left them in the car for hours while he and his girlfriend were in a bar. Once when Alex, my oldest son, was in his teens and completely out of control I called his father to see if he would take him for awhile. He refused. I can't imagine how this must have hurt my son. Their father refused to help two other times: I asked his help to pay for drug/alcohol treatment for Cory and later for college for Jeff. He said drug/alcohol treatment never worked for anyone and he didn't trust that Jeff would stay in college. Many years later, thankfully, he did help when Alex got cancer. But throughout their growing-up years, he was not there for them as a father.

Second marriage

I met my second husband, Carl, at the nursery school where we both took our kids. He had a post-doctorate position at the same college I was attending. He had full custody of his little girl, Abigail, which was unusual at the time. When Abigail was two years old, Carl discovered his wife in an affair, and the courts awarded custody to him. Carl and his ex-wife had been living in Virginia, where he was going to graduate school, but after the divorce, he moved to the state of Washington and took Abigail with him. Abigail spent every summer with her mother, and they called and wrote letters all the time. Her mother did the best she could, living so far away. In all those years we were married I only saw her two times, and I don't remember ever talking with her on the phone. She and Carl handled anything that had to do with Abigail, and I was fine with that.

Before I married her dad I knew Abigail quite well through the nursery school, and my boys knew her, too. I was impressed with Carl as a father. I was touched when Abigail showed me where her dad had patched a rip in her tights. Then one day, he asked if the boys and I wanted to go on a picnic with the two of them. From that time on, we knew we were going to get married, and three months later we did. Both of us had been struggling as single parents. We went for each other like two people dying of thirst on a desert might go for water. It was desperate city.

We were married in the home of a friend of mine whose husband was a minister. We had only two guests—my best friend and Carl's, who were Maid of Honor and Best Man. After our early morning service, we all went to breakfast, and then Carl and I flew off on our honeymoon in his small Super Cub airplane. We camped that night in an area along the Snake River only accessible to hikers and fly-ins. It was pretty romantic, and it was one of the few things we ever did, just the two of us. After that, it was kids, kids, kids

We liked each other; our kids liked each other; we all liked each other. We became this glorious family of six. The boys were five, six and seven, and Abigail was six.

She was absolutely enthralled with me, as I was with her. At last I had a little girl. I sewed dresses for her and put bows in her hair. She would have none of it, ripping the bows from her hair and refusing to remove her cowboy boots even at bedtime. She wanted to be a boy like her new brothers, and the four of them played together all the time. I was disappointed because I had wanted her to be a "girlie girl," but I had to give that up and accept her for who she was. The boys were just happy to have a dad in the house. Initially, it was bliss.

In time, however, the joy ended and problems arose. Two families had married, not a couple. Carl and I had married another parent to help raise children. We weren't passionately in love, but we did like and respect each other. For a number of years we all got along pretty well, putting on happy faces most of the time, but gradually a wall was being constructed between the two families. Often there was an undercurrent of unhappiness. Probably all of us felt it, but I could be wrong. I only know how I felt.

My relationship with my stepdaughter, Abigail

I did not enter this relationship thinking I would be Abigail's real mother. I knew that I would be raising her, but I also knew that she already had a mother, and I was just filling in. But I thought I was "the mother in charge," and I did all the things that mothers do. I was something in between a mother and a stepmother because I mothered her on a daily basis, including disciplining her on the few occasions she needed it. I never asked her to call me Mom, so she has always called me Beth, and that was fine with me. To be truthful, our relationship was more like an aunt and niece.

At first Abigail sort of attached herself to me, but I didn't mind. I remember her telling me about a dream she had. She always had vivid dreams. In her dream "three skinny cowboys" tried to kidnap me while I was doing dishes. In real life my boys were skinny little guys. Maybe she felt she finally had a full-time mother who was being taken away from her. She also became clingy to her father when she realized she had to share him with me and my three sons. Often she had "ear aches" in the night that would require her dad to go in her room and sit with her till she fell asleep.

For me, her mother was sort of out of sight and out of mind. For Abigail, her mother was always in the picture. Sometimes in the early days when Abigail got back from seeing her mother and stepfather, she would rave about all the things she did with them. I remember one time we were in the bathroom, and I was helping wash her hair. She was about nine. I told her she made her dad feel bad when she talked about all the fun things she did with her mother. She didn't really respond; she got quiet. Later when I thought about it, I felt that I shouldn't have said that to her. Maybe I said that because I felt some jealousy, although I don't think I ever felt resentful toward her mother. As Abigail grew older, she kept this part of her life separate and never mentioned much about her mother. She did talk a little about her new brother and sister, but I doubt that she felt like a true part of that family, but then again, we never talked about it.

We did talk about other things. I was fortunate that as she got older we shared a lot of interests such as writing, music and drama. She worked on the middle-school yearbook team with me, and I encouraged her in her writing, which might be why she entered college with a major in journalism. She changed that to science later on. She asked me to try out for parts in a community theater production with her. We both got parts and enjoyed the experience together. We were good friends, more than friends, but not quite mother and daughter.

Her mother came all the way across the country to attend Abigail's high school graduation. She was pleasant, but I do remember feeling a little awkward. When Abigail went to college, her mother finally got her daughter back. She lived with her mom for a year or so before she entered the military. Much later when Abigail lived here in this city, she and her mother and I went to lunch together—Abigail's idea. I think she wanted us to know each other, and I found her mother to be easy to talk to and very likable.

Her father and I divorced when Abigail was in her mid-twenties attending graduate school, but she and I continued to have a relationship. We regularly emailed and talked on the phone. Whenever she was in the area she would always visit and she never forgot a Mother's Day or birthday. Just recently she moved to the city I live in to go to chef's school and we reconnected. On Mother's Day last year she posted on Facebook how lucky she was to have two wonderful mothers.

Carl as a stepdad

Though I had known Abigail for some time before Carl and I got married, he did not know my boys. He barely met them and suddenly he was their stepdad. They were typical rowdy little boys, and Carl had trouble coping with them. They knew he wasn't their real dad and resisted when he tried to discipline them. My oldest even gave him the old "You aren't my dad. You aren't the boss of me." In his own way Carl tried to be a good dad. He became a Cub Scout leader and later a Boy Scout leader. Carl loved Scouting. He's a camper, hiker sort of guy, so doing this wasn't solely for the boys. Only my middle son, Cory, stuck with Scouts. The other two quit right after being Cubs. We also did lots of family backpacking. All of the kids had their own little backpacks and sleeping bags. On our hikes, Carl would name all the plants and trees. He gave each child a book that made each a specialist in one kind of wildlife, like birds, trees, or wild flowers. When we encountered a new specimen, the child with the appropriate book would look it up and tell us about it. Carl also enjoyed woodworking and helped the boys build their own chests of drawers. Carl was a remarkable dad in many ways.

In spite of all the good stuff, Carl initially was a pretty strict disciplinarian. We decided together that all four of the children would have household tasks they were expected to do, things like cleaning their rooms, washing and drying the dishes, and picking up dog doo in the yard. If they failed to do them right, Carl would be upset. He is the kind of person who holds things in, doesn't talk about problems, just grimaces, and then suddenly explodes. Once when Alex and Corey argued over doing the dishes, he grabbed a broom and hit Alex so hard the broom broke. At that time the boys were pretty young; in fact, probably too young to do the dishes. I have a photo of them standing on chairs to reach the sink. I yelled, "Don't you ever touch my children again." From that moment on, he never laid a hand on them. He continued to discipline my boys, but not that way. He grounded them and took privileges away, and I was okay with that. The boys didn't like it, but they accepted it.

Their real dad made the relationship between Carl and the boys even more difficult. He showed up every now and then with presents—once he brought them a mini-motorcycle. He drove a Corvette and always had a good-looking woman with him. Their two fathers couldn't have been more different; the contrast was stark.

In general, our family looked okay, but there was a lot of ugly going on, especially when the boys became teenagers. They started skipping school and partying with their friends. There were car wrecks, arrests for juvenile drinking, even marijuana growing in the closet. Nothing I did seemed to help. Carl stood back and let me handle it for the most part. I was the one who went to the police station to get them when they were in trouble. I was the one who worried and made calls when they missed curfews. Neither of us knew what to do, and Carl sort of gave up. After all, they weren't his children.

I was miserable for a good part of the second half of our marriage. Somehow Carl and I stayed together till well after the kids had all moved out of the house. We raised our kids together, but I wouldn't say we did a good job. Any love we had for each other, and ours had never been a passionate love affair, melted away. The grand plan to unite two families into one failed. I wonder if it's even possible to sew two families together seamlessly. The seams always show, and what you end up with is decidedly different from what you may have imagined. The trick is to give up your illusions and deal with reality the best you can. I guess that's what we did.

How we are today

Today we are all still friends and once in awhile we all still get together. Our divorce was amicable, and in some ways we still carry on the idea that ours was a happy family. We come together for graduations and holidays and keep fairly close track of each other.

Abigail seemed to do better than the boys. At least she didn't act out as the boys did, but I'm sure she was affected. After serving a term in the US Air Force, she finished college and then went into veterinarian school. She graduated with honors and worked as a vet for a number of years. Her interests changed, and recently she graduated from chef school. She married while she was in the Air Force, and though they were married for many years they never had kids. Her husband was an older guy who already had kids and didn't want any more. Abigail loves animals, so she has always had lots of dogs and cats. They divorced after over twenty years of marriage.

All three boys graduated from community colleges and are certificated in trades: Alex and Jeff in auto body repair and Cory in heating/air conditioning. They did not choose academic careers as Carl did, but instead went for the skilled trades as their father did. Cory and Alex have been married and divorced. Jeff has been married for many years but has no children, though they wanted them.

Carl has always been especially good to Cory, my middle son. He considers Cory's two daughters (both graduated from college now) his granddaughters and has been good to them throughout their lives. Jim tried to mend fences with the boys in his older years and has been a pretty good grandfather to his granddaughters. His relationship with all three of his sons remains somewhat tense, and he has almost no relationship with Alex.

Reflections

I really hate divorce, especially when children are involved. It always affects the children adversely in my opinion. Sure, they weather it, but it always leaves scars. I also know that in some cases, there is little choice but to divorce. I divorced the father of my children because he was constantly cheating with other women, drinking and partying, completely unreliable. It was the hardest thing I ever did because I truly loved him. I filed for divorce three times, always going back to try again, but I finally realized nothing was going to change. I remember the marriage counselor telling me, "Well, you have two choices—you can leave him or you can stay with him and put up with his behavior. Some men quit cheating when they get older." It's some consolation to know that he never did quit. He is now sixty-nine years old and still cheating on his long-suffering third wife who has chosen to stay with him anyway. They have no children. Neither my first husband nor I had any more children.

Considering this, my first piece of advice should be "Choose your marriage partners carefully." I married for love the first time. I chose with my heart. It didn't work out. The second time I married, I chose with my head. I knew what I didn't want—a drinker, a cheater. I chose a man who seemed to be a good father. He was honest, faithful and true, and he was intelligent. He had a PhD in biology and a good job at a university. He was like a perfect Boy Scout. How could things go wrong? But they did.

So what advice can I offer? I guess you need to choose with both your head and your heart, and if you have children, do not divorce unless you absolutely have to. Work it out if you can. Strangely, even though the children had been out of the house for a long time when I divorced my second husband, it still hurt them. The family was broken—again. Also, give yourself plenty of time to get to know each other before you remarry. If we had done this, we might not have married.

Secondly, try to love your stepchildren as your own. Work at it, if it doesn't come naturally. They are innocents in this whole thing. All they want is to be loved and cared for. I've always loved Abigail, still do, yet the love I have for her is different from the love I have for my sons. The bond is different; maybe it's a biological thing. I know she has a mother and a father who love her well, and I think that makes a difference, too. There were times in our relationship when we drifted apart. I'm sure we had some jealousies, on both our parts probably, but I really think they faded over time. Carl has admitted being somewhat jealous of my boys; this was in parent counseling when Cory went through drug/alcohol treatment. I never knew till then. It's a hard thing to admit.

Last, but maybe the most important: Insist on the child support whether you need it or not. Not only will it come in handy later in the children's lives, but throughout the years they will see that the other parent cares about them, if only through the payments he/she makes each month.

Sometimes I wonder if it would have been better for my sons if I had not married the second time. Perhaps I should have tried to raise them on my own. But when I consider all aspects, I realize that I did what I thought was best for all of us. We did form a family and, though it wasn't perfect, what family is? If you talk to the kids today, they'll tell you they have no complaints about the way we raised them.

Though there were all kinds of heartaches each of us in the family carried, for the most part we hid them from each other. I guess what we did was what some counselors tell you to do: "Act as if." Act as if you are happy when you aren't and pretty soon you will be. Maybe. There were too many factors working against us, but I think we all tried. I remember one Christmas when my son Alex was so delighted with everything. He was about nine I think. He looked at me, his little face beaming, and said, "I want all of us to always have Christmas together like this forever." Even with divorce, we still do.

Mark and Fran's Stories

Mark has two children, a boy and girl, Susan and Steve. Fran has two, a boy and a girl, David and Pat. Mark and Fran are now grandparents with ten grandchildren.

Mark's Story

What does family mean to you?

I don't view family as people just getting together and living in a home. Families share goals and values. Fran and I are basically two families coming together, and we created one family from that.

My mother was born in Eastern Europe and came over right after the First World War. My father's family was born in Russia, but my father was born here after most of his family had come over. Essentially, I had two Eastern European parents. They were not well educated. They didn't have much; they had to work as young kids. My father was in the liquor store business and retail markets, but for most of his life he was in the wholesale produce business. He would have to get up early in the morning, so I didn't see a lot of him because he was asleep earlier than we were and got up earlier. I didn't have a terribly close relationship with my father, much more with my mother. They were strict in certain ways, but they gave me a lot of latitude to do what I wanted. My mother had four brothers and sisters that we would see frequently. I was not close to my grandparents because there was a language barrier: they spoke Yiddish. My kids maintained a relationship with my mother and father. We would visit them regularly.

Divorce and meeting Fran

When my wife and I separated, my kids, Susan and Steve, stayed with me every other weekend, and I saw them one night during the week. The one night of the week I would pick them up and we would go to dinner. In those days video games, like Pac Man, were popular, so we would often go to a video store, and during the weekends we would try to do different things. I lived at the beach so they would have the ability to go to the beach.

I originally got an apartment a block away from my ex-wife's place, and then I moved, but I was still relatively close. The hardest thing was to stay in contact with the kids because I didn't see them every day. They were with me every other weekend and once during the week. We never varied. It was religious. The kids were incredibly good about it. I don't remember ever having any opposition, although I think it was difficult for them too, but they just accepted the fact that that was the routine. They would call me; I would call them. It's hard because you are not physically with them.

I had been dating for a year when I met Fran, and we hit it off immediately. We continued to go out regularly thereafter. When we met, her son David was six, her daughter Pat and my daughter Susan were nine, and my son Steve was ten. At a point, I'm guessing within a year and a half, I moved in with her. In those days when I had my kids I would be with Fran and her kids. I typically wouldn't go off alone with my kids after Fran and I got serious. Maybe I should have.

The families were very much together very early, which is not to say that everyone always got along well. It was a lot of work to be with the kids and be concerned about jealousies and so forth. But my kids were great and so were hers. By and large it worked out pretty well. We decided in those early days not to have any more children. That was a conscious decision. We thought we had great kids: two boys, two girls, all healthy. We were looking forward to them growing up and four was enough.

Fran and I would always have Wednesday nights alone together because her kids would go with her ex-husband. Wednesday night was kind of a ritual. That was just a known thing. The kids were unbelievably good about this. Some kids might rebel, but my kids never really did nor did hers. Sometimes we had every other weekend together as well, but that really didn't happen much because the kids were around or one of the other parents was on vacation.

Fran's life changed significantly because of my involvement with her. She had a very difficult divorce. Her husband was still around and still certainly affected them, but I think it would have been much worse had I not been there. I was a stabilizing influence. I had a better relationship with him than Fran did in those early years.

My ex-wife remarried. Fran and I would see them from time to time at family events. We were cordial but never sought a close relationship. I never could quite understand how people could continue to have these cozy relationships with their former husbands and wives. Some do.

Making one family out of two

Every other weekend the four kids were together. David, the youngest, was a focal point for everyone. My son is very personable, and he and David seemed to get along very well. I don't remember fighting or big scenes. Bottom line all the kids seemed to pretty much get along well together. It didn't happen initially, but a few years after we got married they would refer to each other as brother and sister as opposed to stepbrother and stepsister.

My kids always had a special place at our house. They viewed it not as the other guy's home, but their home as well. When Fran and I bought our house, we demolished the inside and re-did it to make it into a home for all of us. The kids were a part of all that. We rebuilt the house in large part with them in mind. The boys had their own rooms, and the girls shared a large room where they each had their own bed and a big work/study area. We had a pretty normal existence when my kids were with us. We ate in a lot which I think was a good thing. Fran is a big believer in that.

We always tried to do a lot of things together as a family. We traveled with the kids frequently. We traded off holidays with the other parents. We became a family because we were all together so often. We've had a number of family trips recently with the four kids and our grandkids, and everyone got along unbelievably well.

We didn't marry for approximately three years. I would have married a year earlier, but Fran thought we should wait. We did something that was pretty dangerous—we didn't tell the kids we were getting married. We asked them to join us for a holiday trip to Hawaii, and when they arrived we invited them to our wedding the next day. There were just the six of us. We kind of eloped. Nobody else was there at the wedding, just them, so it was special.

The relationships among our four kids have grown stronger over the years. Three of them went to the same college. Today David lives in the same city as my daughter Susan, and they see a lot of each other, and Steve is in constant contact with all three of the other kids.

Our roles as parents and stepparents

Fran and I were pretty similar in our parenting philosophy. We were relatively laissez faire; we kind of let them do their own thing. Not a lot of pressure from us, but they had to be home at a certain time; they had to be in bed by a certain time; they had to do their homework. We were pretty easy in terms of bending the rules when they needed to be bent. By and large we tended to discipline our kids separately, but we did weigh in from time to time which sometimes I'm sure created issues, but we wanted to make sure we were consistent. Consistency is very important. That is true even in a normal relationship, but it is harder when you have a divorce situation.

My best recollection is that I didn't really have any issue with Fran's kids. They were pretty accepting from the beginning, but that could be my rose-colored glasses. When we first started dating I was just a boyfriend, but I never remember them being anything but accepting. The only thing I tried very consciously to do was not be their father. They had a father. I was not there to replace him. I never saw myself as their friend either. I was an adult who was involved with their mother and married their mother. Not that I didn't love them, but I never asked them to call me Dad or anything like that. Neither of us professed to be the other children's parent. She was Fran and I was Mark. We were the adults, the husband of their mother or the wife of their father, so we were parent-like persons but not a mother or father. This is a hard line and we were careful not to cross that line.

I always tried to make my kids understand that they were my kids and that the other two were not my children but that I was very close to them and loved them too. If there was ever an issue I would try to make it clear that they were my kids. That's a hard one because they knew how close I was to Fran's kids. Every once in awhile, I recall being concerned about that. My guess is that they probably still have those feelings in terms of our relationship with their kids, our grandkids, although Fran and I have always been very careful to get close to all of our grandchildren. By and large, I don't think the grandchildren see any difference and accept the fact that we love them all equally.

Fran had a few more issues initially with my kids than I had with hers. I lived with her kids, so I would see them more often; that might be part of it. Susan was very close to her mom, which perhaps made it more difficult for her, but whenever we had the kids she always came. Unlike Steve who lived with us his senior year of high school, she didn't move in until after she graduated from college, mainly because of concerns she had about her mother, how she would react. Susan had a boyfriend (her future husband) who was going to graduate school near us. She was working while he was in school, and she would go back and forth a lot between his apartment and our home. They would often have dinner with us, which was a very nice way to get closer. It was good to be with my daughter, and especially good for Fran and Susan. They really bonded. Today Fran is as close to my daughter as I am, or maybe closer.

After a number of years Fran and I became so close with each other's kids, and there was a love there that was so strong, that we were kind of their mother or father. Every once in a while, for example, Pat would introduce me as her dad as opposed to her stepfather. The stepchild, stepfather, stepmother labels were almost never used, which is interesting. I think we didn't even feel that way. Ultimately, I wasn't a stepfather and Fran wasn't a stepmother, but we still weren't their actual mother or father. We were certainly a very close substitute.

As Steve went through his teenage years, when there were issues, I was typically the one to handle them. I think Fran felt a little left out of that relationship for awhile. I remember having some issues early on between him and Fran but not serious problems at all. It was a matter of feeling each other out. Fran's relationship with him has varied from time to time, but has become stronger and stronger. It is very solid today, and they are very close.

The grandkids call Fran, Nonna, which is Italian for grandmother. That happened a long time ago but initially there was a distinction I guess because Fran wasn't their natural grandparent. My son's kids, who were our first grandkids, called her Fran at first. Now all the grandkids call her Nonna. I'm sure none of them view her any differently; maybe they are even closer to her because we really became a family for all the kids. Today our kids and the grandkids call us Papa and Nonna.

Reflections

Fran and I have always had a really wonderful relationship, and I do think a lot of it has to do with the fact that we insisted on having time together alone. Most people don't have that luxury. When we had our Wednesday nights, that was probably the only time during the week when we were alone. We guarded that and it became a ritual. Our Wednesday nights became sacred to us. That's one of the reasons we have such a strong relationship.

Also important is that we really tried to be very even-handed with all four kids. I'm not sure that all the kids feel that way, but we tried. We wanted to create a family of all six of us, and eventually we became the nuclear family separate from their other mothers and fathers. We traveled a lot together and that helped. We rarely spoke poorly of the other parents, and that helped too. We just tried to treat each child as if he or she were ours, with a little extra understanding regarding the sensitivity for our own kids. We tried over the years to make sure that all the kids felt that we cared for them. I think that happened. But you never know. You try not to play favorites, but then you try not to play favorites with your own kids as well. There could be lots of things I may not be appreciating here. Now it is somewhat more difficult because they have different situations, but you try to be responsible for whatever needs arise.

I think the hard line is to treat all the kids equally. It's much harder when you have two families coming together to make sure that your own children understand that you love them even though you may also love your spouse's children. What I tried to do sometimes was to make my own children feel a little more special without detracting from the way I felt about Fran's kids. That is a very hard thing to do, and my guess is that it doesn't work for most people. We tried to treat the kids equally without impacting upon the love that our own children felt for us and we felt for them. My perceptions could be all wrong if you asked the kids.

Fran and I have always tried to be accommodating to the needs of the kids. I tended to basically say, "Do what makes you feel comfortable. If you need to see your mom, go ahead and do that." Often they would come to town and see their mother and not us. But I knew how close they were with us.

For me, the biggest reward of being a stepdad has been the variety of the kids. They are all different. I come from a very small family, so having four kids and all these grandchildren is paradise. I was essentially an only child. My brother was twelve years older, so he was pretty much out of the house as I was growing up, so for me to have a large family was kind of fun, something I wasn't used to. They all have different moods, different objectives, and different personalities. It's just amazing. It's great watching them grow up. We've been really fortunate, I must say.

Fran's Story

What does family mean to you?

Family can be a mix of a lot of different things. It is like art. You know it when you see it and feel it. Families care about each other and take care of each other. They get mad at each other, but not often. What I feel about family has been there forever and was made clearer to me when my mother died. I saw how close we were. My mother had a real sense of family and emphasized being a good person, doing the right thing for people. I offered Mark the commitment to family my mother taught me.

I'm from a large family. I have one brother and three sisters and there was always room for different personalities. My parents both had very good educations and always stressed education. My father was quiet and my mother was very outgoing. She was interested in many subjects: ballet, music, education. They had a very beautiful social life. They took extraordinary trips and often included us in those trips, which was unusual at that time for a family with five children. We went to Mexico a number of times; we went to Europe, and many other places.

My mother always enjoyed being a mother and a wife and was crazy about my father. When we were very young, I remember my mom asking what we wanted to be when we grew up. Each of us answered that we wanted to be a parent. That was the 50s. Women's concepts of their roles changed in the 60s. My father traveled a lot, but we always had dinner together. There wasn't any question—we had dinner together. I did that with my kids too. I remember thinking, "You don't start dinner until everyone sits down."

Divorce and finding myself

I was married in the 1960s. I was very young. I was nineteen, finished college and worked as a social worker. Then I had Pat when I was twenty-three and David three years later. My husband and I separated after fourteen years of marriage when I was in my early thirties. Our divorce was difficult and there was a lot of anger. That was a bad time, and it lasted for a long time.

My divorce was about getting a sense of my own identity. The women's movement was taking off. This was an exciting time when women were becoming more involved, a time of developing one's self. A lot of us went back to work. My sister and many of my friends were becoming lawyers and going into other professions. I wanted to be an example for my children of someone who was self-sufficient, so in the early 70s I went back to school to study art history. That was a real awakening and I felt very strong. Later I developed a business around art. Going back to school and working again really changed things for me. By the way, this was the 60s and 70s, and today for many women I do not think it is a choice of whether or not to return to the workforce but a necessity.

I started my art business out of my home that was designed with an office for me and racks to hold inventory. I would hang art on the walls in my home giving people the opportunity to see artwork in a home environment. I had exhibitions three to four times a year and later opened a gallery. I loved having the gallery. Preparing for an exhibition was like an on-going education. I loved meeting the clients and artists. I did this for many years and recently retired. Now I am exhausted from all the wonderful things Mark and I do.

Meeting Mark and developing a relationship

Soon after I separated, I began going out with Mark. Neither Mark nor I remember our first date, but it might have been a Woody Allen film. I was an independent, professional person when he met me. He was interested in what I did and what I had to say. Mark has always been a good listener. I remember feeling very empowered by this. I especially remember that we had so many interesting things to talk about—music, art, social issues—and we shared the same values.

Mark is four years older than I am, and it's funny how those four years make a difference. He is definitely part of the 50s, where I feel much more part of the 60s. Mark is really the best part of the 50s. He did succeed in school and believes in the American Dream that by doing well in school and working hard, you can prosper. Everybody to this day is proud of Mark and knows that he was very proud of his education. His father worked into the wee hours in the produce market, so a lot of what Mark did accomplish was on his own. He believes each of us has this ability.

By the time I met Mark I was working and had a much better sense of myself. I wanted my children to see me with someone who respected me, and I just knew he was somebody who was respectful of women. I was thrilled to develop myself, and Mark was one wonderful part of that. He was so encouraging. I remember expressing that I was giving my children the gift of a good example. I knew this right away. He sought out somebody who was independent, who could be an intellectual partner, and he was so pleased that I was independent and working. My generation went to college, had our children, went back to school, and evolved into some other kind of person, and those were the people Mark and I were when we met each other.

Mark and I were crazy about each other, and each of us thought the other was the kind of person we wanted our children to know and appreciate. This made for a very good relationship. From the beginning, we had almost every other weekend and every Wednesday night together. We institutionalized this time. We were so excited to meet each other as individuals, and that was the time we could be those individuals. If you can, create a regular time when you are alone together. Get away from everybody. That is your time. This is good advice for everyone.

Mark and I as parents and stepparents

I think it was a couple of months after we met that I met Mark's children. He invited me and my children to join them at a baseball game. Our children were around the same age, with the boys as bookends. We always took our kids with us. If I went skiing, I would always take my kids. They always came along. The same with Mark.

Mark was a very committed dad. He cherished his time with his kids, and they knew it. I don't think his kids ever thought that he was my kid's father, and my kids didn't think that either. They had their own father. They never said, "You're not my dad. You can't do that." My kids always really respected him. When Mark said something, it was taken seriously. He helped give more structure and discipline, and I think the children liked that. While I am the kind of person who says, "I'm upset," Mark is the kind who says, "Let's sit down and figure out what to do." He addresses issues, but not in a negative way. He is a pretty smart guy, and all through the years he is the one who has been a problem-solver. He has a calm and rational mind. Mark was the rock.

In the beginning, I think Mark's daughter Susan and I felt threatened by each other. Mark and I were crazy about each other, and it was hard for me to share him. Here is a young child, and dad is with another woman. For Susan it probably became "How do you show your loyalty to your mom when there is someone else?" Now that I look back on this, of course, this young girl thinks, "Who is this woman that my dad is so smitten with?" I met her when she was ten years old. Then she became a teenager and then grew up and came to live with us after college. She could say at that point, "Mom, I have lived with you all these years. I would like to try to live a year or two with my dad." It seemed fair. This was an amazing thing to do because of her loyalty to her mom. It was enormous.

That was a magical time. Without the other children around, she and I had the opportunity to really enjoy each other. I realize how much of my family experience touches around dinner, which I think is hilarious since I am not a good cook. After work we would always meet back and have dinner together. Sometimes it was just Susan, Mark and I at the table, but also what was so wonderful was that Lawrence, who became Susan's husband, would so often have dinner with us. We were able to develop a wonderful relationship with him. That was really a fabulous brew that the four of us had. Susan and I are now extremely close.

Steve has always been very close to Mark, and so when he wanted to spend his last year of high school with us, it was probably easier for his mom to say, "Okay do it," and I think Steve knew that too. We always talk about the parent having special time with the child, but for a stepparent to have special time with the child is extraordinary. I come from a large family and loved the idea of Mark's kids living with us. We had built our house with that in mind. There were times, though when I felt that I was being excluded. When there was a problem, Mark would go into Steve's room to talk and I was left out. I thought, "If he's living here, I have to be a part of this." It felt isolating; not that I should be the parent in charge, but I felt that I was a person, a part of his life and part of the environment. That was brought to a head and resolved. I finally said, "I'm feeling left out here. What am I?" This came down to Mark acknowledging it and saying, "Okay we'll change."

When I didn't handle something right, I never felt that this defined me. Sometimes the worst part is that you feel embarrassed. Looking back I realize that there were so many times I must have been hard on Mark's children. Now I realize, number one, I was so young, and two, I must have been jealous. It's so interesting to go back and learn that you were not as good as you thought you were, but Mark never made me feel that I was being a bad person. He always found what it was that I was trying to say and supported me. Even if I did do things I wish I had done differently, I don't carry a lot of baggage. We got through it. Things didn't stop there.

Pulling our two families together

Our day-to-day life was done in a conscious way. Being together at dinner time was the glue. We bought a house that could handle all our children, and they could see that house as their family home. The boys each had their own room, and the girls decided to share one large space, even though it was designed to have two bedrooms. Mark and I were so excited to do things together, and we wanted our children to join in. We spent a lot of time together as a family. We created adventures and organized activities. We were lucky that sports were a big part of their lives, and we went to their games. We really did not believe in being couch potatoes.

We also traveled a lot with the children. Not everyone can afford to do this; we were fortunate. Mark and I are both passionate about travel, and he arranges the most amazing trips. One of our most memorable experiences was when we all went to Kenya and Tanzania for three weeks. We all fit into one Range Rover, and a lot of the time we were bumping all over the roads. Mark and I were like flies on the wall and were so privileged to hear the kids in the back seat discussing and arguing about different subjects such as women's issues, politics, etc. There was no television and there were times we slept in tents. We all brought books but David decided he wasn't going to bring any. We were all reading one of those mystery books. David wanted to know how the book ended and no one would tell him, so he had to read the book himself. Steve is so good at dramatizing and telling stories. He has this twinkling personality and he loves to be on stage. He provided great entertainment retelling his crazy dreams. We all loved it. This trip was so wonderful. I don't think things can ever be 100 percent, but experiences together create memories. It's material to work with. You sit around and say, "Do you remember when . . .?"

By the time we got married the feeling was, finally you are doing what you are supposed to be doing. We had been living together for three years before we got married, which gave us room to catch up with ourselves. All of us. There is no escape valve when you live with people. The marriage thing was much more important for Mark, and as it has turned out, it was a wonderful thing. Marriage wasn't what I was looking for. I thought, "I've already done that. Why do I want to do that again? We have it all; why mess it up with getting married?" But Mark put his foot down, and I didn't push the envelope. It was such a good decision. The kids had seen us as a family for a long time. We got married in Hawaii where we were vacationing with the kids, but they didn't know that we were planning to get married there. We were married in the chapel in a synagogue, just the six of us, and then we went out for a lovely lunch at a restaurant. I believe that my kids knew that this was the right marriage for me.

Our lives were so full we decided not to have any more children. We felt that each of us had two healthy children, and we didn't have the need to have more. We were satisfied with what we had. I also remember thinking that even though I am pro-choice, if I get pregnant I wouldn't so easily get an abortion. I don't think we thought there was something missing. Some women think, "If I had a child with him we would have the same glue and story and memories."

Our family today

Parenting never stops. Even though Mark and I are older, these relationships are ongoing and can change. We have always been very close. I hate to brag, and I am also superstitious, but I feel that at this time we are a very strong and loving family. I believe the four children see each other as an integral family and that they really feel like brothers and sisters.

Our children all have different economic situations. Mark never said, "Those are your kids." All the kids know that we are there for all of them, and they are aware of the financial needs of the others. If we need to help, we help. We bring an even hand. This continues because the world has changed. Many of my friends are involved with helping their children today. That is just the way it is. That can be a real challenge, but Mark and I understand that the kids are hard-working people. This is just a different time.

All of our children married very young. Pat and David each have three children, and Steve and Susan each have two. Both Mark and I have very special places in all four children's lives and our grandchildren's lives. Steve was the first one to have children. Originally the two other mothers were the grandmothers, and I stayed in the background. But then I finally said, "You know what? I adore these kids and I want to be a part of their lives." It really became—What is my role? One day when Pat was about to have her first child, she turned to me and said, "You guys go to Italy every summer; you will be known as Nonna." I always laugh when I think about this because that name was as new to me as it was to them. As the other children had our grandchildren, they started to call me Nonna. Steve and his children also started to call me Nonna. Finally we had a word. Instead of calling me Fran, Nonna was a loving word that defines who I am. All of a sudden, who I was became very comfortable for all of them.

Mark and I try to be close to each of the four families. Aside from big events, we make a conscious effort to regularly visit each family or have them visit us. We've had some spectacular times with everyone, but I also find it just wonderful to be with one family or just the kids when it's much more concentrated and focused. For example, David's family skied with us a couple of weeks ago, and Susan and Pat's families skied with us in March. What a thrill. We are going to Chicago to go to art galleries with Susan and her husband. We try to help out with Pat's childcare needs because both parents work. We love to visit with Steve's family to see our grandson play football and be there when our granddaughter comes home from college for visits. It's just time together; loving these kids and letting them know that we are there to help. I learned that if you don't make a point of going to see the kids, to show the interest and spend the time, there is a message there. In this day and age it is expensive and difficult for families to travel, so Mark and I make an effort to get to our children. No one lives close by, and our children would understand if we didn't. But it's important to visit. I make that happen. You've got to walk the walk.

Reflections

I brought to Mark's kids someone who loved their father and would take care of their father, and that is a great sense of comfort. They really know that. Mark and I are an example of a successful and loving marriage. Also, they could see me as someone who worked and carried her own weight. They saw my relationship with my own family, and on some level that played into their understanding of who I was. My mother always remembered their birthdays, and when she passed away she accommodated for them in her will. They know they are a part of my family.

There aren't too many great things about getting older, but one of the best is to know that you can go through something, and there is a start, a middle, and you can get to the other side. You can make mistakes. and you can also get through the mistakes. Today I am able to say to my stepdaughter Susan, "I love you," and she will say, "I know," which is better than the automatic "I love you, too." We all keep growing. The greatest joy of being a stepmom is love. It sounds saccharine, but I love my stepkids so much and they love me, and I really know that. People keep trying to define their roles as stepparents, but you can't anticipate them. Relationships evolve. Maybe the gift is to know that things do work out. As my dad used to say, “Let’s just go out and take a ride.”

What is the role of a stepmother? If anyone needs something, provide it. If anyone wants to talk, talk with them. If they don’t feel like talking, accept that and respect that. If you see them doing something wrong, say, “Hey, you’re doing something wrong.” When the children are with you, these are people that you help take care of. It’s the same feeling I have for my own children. You are there to be there for them, but don’t expect children who barely know you to necessarily love you right away just because their father tells them he is in love with you. Love evolves.

Mark and I continue to be crazy for each other and we are a great support to each other. At all times this relationship has been a very reassuring part of my life. I asked Mark, “Did you ever in all these years think that this wouldn’t work out?” He said, “No. That never went through my mind.” So much is luck. It’s organic. I wish I had a recipe book. But I don’t.

Tonia's Story

Tonia married Brian when she was thirty-six. Brian has two daughters, Donna and Christie, from his first marriage. They did not have any children together.

What Does Family Mean to You?

I think of family as the people you choose or who have chosen you, or those you're thrown into life with. They're the people you try to protect and shelter and stick with, those who bring you hopefully the most joy, but often pain too, thc people that really are your little tribe. They're the ones that give you the catch and the throw, the people you will do anything for. It's unlike relationships you have with anybody else.

The interesting thing about family is that you normalize what you grow up with. I grew up in the 50s and 60s with a Mexican father and an American mother. I had two parents who stayed together. My mother's parents lived together long-term, and everybody was heterosexual or so I thought, and everybody was going to get married and have babies. That's what I saw. That was formative to me. Our family was really close. We got together with my American cousins every Sunday, and we spent a lot of time with my grandparents. Family was that group of people who loved me, who cared about me, and was fierce about that, and that is what I expected we owed to each other. I think I grew up pretty secure that way. That informs how I feel about family today.

I have had friends who had very dysfunctional biological families, and they have chosen networks of friends to be their families. The whole society is so different. People aren't necessarily married or aren't all heterosexual, and relationships fluctuate. My own adult relationships have been serial and numerous, and they are all family to me. The definition expands. That is why the central core of my view is that family are the people to whom you feel fiercely connected.

Growing up

My father emigrated from Mexico in the late 1920s or early 1930s. He was poor on arrival and worked his way through school and became a college professor during the depression years. He was a hard-working, bootstraps kind of man. He met my mother in Oakland when he was in his thirties and she was just twenty. When my mother was twelve, she decided she wanted to marry a Mexican. Her family loved Mexico. She majored in Spanish, and by the time she met my father she was fluent in Spanish.

My father came to America not speaking any English and had a pretty rough time. He lived in the South and Midwest before coming to California. My mother dropped out of college when she married, like many women in her generation. My father was not a citizen yet, so he volunteered to serve during WWII. They were separated for some years while he was in the service. She had already had my oldest brother Marcos during that time, and then the other two of us were born later. I was born in 1949 and that is the year they moved to the house I grew up in, so I never knew any other family home. My brother Marcos is six years older than I am, and my brother Frankie is two years older. My mother never worked outside the home except sometimes she would help my dad, or sometimes she would substitute teach when the nuns were sick. She was a homemaker and so was her mother who was married to a dentist, my grandpa.

I was very close to my American side of the family which included my grandparents and my aunt, my mother's only sibling, and her family. They lived in the same area and we saw a lot of one another. I really loved my Mexican side of the family, but we didn't see them very often. When I was a little kid, some of my cousins would come and live with us during the school year. My father grew more and more involved in his career as a doctor, publishing and lecturing internationally, and was absent much of the time. My grandfather was more fatherly than my father, so we were lucky to have him.

My father was a conservative republican all his life and all the rest of us were of a different political mindset. He was very pro-military and pro-republican, but he liked the Kennedys because they were Catholic. He was in denial about experiencing discrimination. It was too much cognitive dissonance for him. But my mom has told me that there were people who disrespected him and people who would not rent to them because he was Mexican, even though he was an educated and well-respected guy in his profession.

My mother's sister, my Aunt Pat, had a big impact on me. I grew up with two distinct cultural views about children. My father's expectations were extremely high and extremely specific, whereas Aunt Pat and my grandpa were very flexible. Their view was that kids are not your extensions. While my Aunt Pat became a dentist like her dad, none of her kids went to college and that was okay with her.

My parents expected me to go to a good college and have a career. I was expected to work and use my mind. I was brought up thinking that I could do anything my brothers could do, unusual for a young Latina. At first I went to college to become a bilingual science teacher because I wanted girls to learn science and I wanted to teach barrio youth. I changed direction in my fifth year of college and decided to become a doctor. I went through medical school on a public health service scholarship, and in return I worked in an underserved area. I never called what I did a career. Terms like *career* or *profession* were anathema to me. I was averse to that because of my own politics. I was a hippie.

Meeting my husband

I always had relationships and considered myself likely to be with somebody, but I didn't think about marriage and didn't marry until I was thirty-six. And that was in the face of a lot of pressure from my Mexican family. My godmother, who was my beloved aunt, used to pray that I would please stop being a *solterona* (a very old maid). My long-term dream was to travel around the country and scout out where I wanted to live.

I was at the start of that trip when I met my future husband, Brian. I met him in Washington where he was visiting mutual friends. He had been married to a woman named Adele, and they had two children, Donna and Christie. He was seventeen when Donna was born. They lived in the farmlands of Othello, Washington, where he worked in construction. After Christie was born, they moved to rural Colorado. They bought some land and built a house and lived there awhile. When the kids were five and three, they separated amicably. Adele was glad to see him go. She had a boyfriend in the wings. Christie doesn't remember anything about it, but Donna remembers a lot. She remembers her father's departure. It was a huge moment for her.

Brian and Adele were happy to be divorced. They had no regrets. The only reason they were in touch was the kids. Adele had sole custody of the girls, but she never objected to his taking them on weekends or on trips. Hippie culture helped here. It wasn't cool to be jealous. Lots of people were having serial relationships, and lots of people were wandering around trying to find themselves. Brian became an itinerant hippie and hitchhiked around the country and Canada. He took up with another woman named Theresa whom he later married, and they went to live for a time close to his two daughters. Theresa was quite involved with the girls. I think the world of her. She is not a "child person," so it's amazing that she did that. The memory of her is important to the girls.

Meeting my stepdaughters

Brian and I were in Wyoming. We were preparing to start out the next day for Florida, but he woke up and said, "I think I need to see the girls. I think we need to live close to them." I didn't even know where that place in rural Colorado was but I was quite happy to hear that, although I was worried because he got so specific about where we would live. It turned out that it was a great place to live, although I didn't have a job for awhile, and it has always been a challenge since then to create the kind of work I like and that suits my personality. It is a small town and there are not too many options.

Brian didn't prepare me at all to meet his kids. I don't

think he knew them very well. When I heard he had kids, it was an attractive thing to me, but when he talked about them, he seemed somewhat naïve about them and that made me wary of him. That was a big deal. Later I learned he was indeed very attached, but scared of being involved in their lives, and he needed a partner who could help him.

Brian wrote to the girls that we were coming for a visit. That's all he told them. I was nervous. It was a beautiful spring weekend where they lived. When we arrived at Adele and her husband Danny's, the girls came running out, jumping all over their dad, really excited with big smiles. They said, "You must be Antonia," which is what he called me at first. "We've heard so much about you." They were extremely welcoming.

Donna was fourteen and Christie was twelve. I later learned from Christie they thought that any girlfriend or wife of their dad was great because they softened him, despite the fact that I knew he was a big marshmallow. He was just this guy who didn't go for any small talk or any ordinary customs and who seemed very serious to them.

When I first met my stepdaughters, I was a novelty. I was the new girlfriend and later the new wife but not the first one they had encountered. They definitely spoke of me as their stepmother even before we were married. They seemed to be happy with that term and that idea. I think if they had lived with us it would have been quite different, but because they were visitors in our home and their dad was quite intense in those years, they regarded me as an ally. They felt safe with me and like many women, I am better at small talk, going out for errands, the small daily things. I would take them shopping, something guys aren't generally good at. We'd always go thrift-store shopping which they thought was fun and liked. Now as adults (and moms) themselves, they're big thrift-store shoppers.

I wanted to spend time with my stepdaughters, and Brian always encouraged that. He didn't observe traditional holidays, so he had never sent them Christmas or birthday presents. I was totally scandalized. The first year, I sewed Christmas stockings which we still use. He thought that was funny, but he went along with a lot of things that were not natural to him but that were my ideas for creating family traditions. Every Christmas it became a tradition to give each of the girls a present that was just from me. I gave them each a copy of *Our Body Ourselves* when they were fifteen. Those were years at the beginning when we hardly had any money, so gifts were always modest, but there was always this other special gift from me to open. I think they liked that.

The girls are very different in temperament. We had to really reach out to Donna at times—she would withdraw into her own world. Although I didn't know her as a little girl, Brian tells me that Donna was introverted and introspective even as a toddler. She had some very rough times as a child and teen. She was a very beautiful girl, a knock-out. Once I asked Donna how it felt when she heard that her dad was going to move back to be with her. She said, "He's coming back in the nick of time. I think if it had been any later, I would never have forgiven him." It was a very dramatic statement.

When we arrived, Christie was still a little girl physically. Men didn't notice her for a long time even though she really wanted them to. She was extroverted, resilient, bubbly and desperate for her sister's affection, which was not forthcoming when they were young. She was really excited that her dad was in town, and she wanted to live with us fulltime. Theirs was such a different relationship from the one I had with my own dad. Even at the age of twelve, she would crawl into his lap and want him to cuddle her. She just ate up his attention and love. It was impressive how much she wanted him in her life.

Parenting with Danny and Adele

I've always liked Adele. I find her to be very serene, which is a quality I don't have and like to be around when I'm with other women. She is an ethical person. I am a doctor and she is a nurse, and we have been able to share things about our work. Her family is salt of the earth. They completely welcomed us, even though they'd earlier had grudges against Brian for "leaving their daughter." They accepted our move to the area with enthusiasm. We were all family. It was amazing to me.

Danny is a really good person and a wonderful stepdad. He took on a huge amount to live with a woman with two teenagers. Brian and I have great respect for him. He set good boundaries and convinced Adele to move back to a quiet place. It was a good place to raise the girls. He rescued them all. But the girls fought him like crazy. They love their mom a lot, and he was the interloper. They saw Danny as the big, bad disciplinarian and when Brian came back into the picture, they embraced him. Danny was jealous of Brian. He says over and over again how he did all the grunt work of raising the girls. And it's true. Danny and I bonded on one thing. When Donna was going through risky behavior in high school, Adele and Brian, the biological parents, would believe her stories.

Danny and I would just shake our heads. We had much more of a disciplinarian approach, where her biological parents were softies.

For the most part, Brian and I didn't rock the boat with his daughters. That was good in many ways because it helped create a happy bond that persists. It wasn't as meaningful as I now wish it had been in terms of really taking more of a role in things like helping the girls with school or helping them articulate goals, or avoid risky behaviors. I just didn't get into that mix very much. And neither really did Brian. He was reentering their lives with some trepidation, and we both felt that a lot of respect needed to be shown to their mom and Danny because they were raising them. Now looking back I see that we had a very light touch and not as much concern as we needed to have about some things in the girls' lives, and when we did show concern we always deferred to their mom and stepdad.

Some of the things we failed to do amounted to a betrayal of the kids, I now believe. For the girls to have understood that they had at least their dad and me really concerned about certain behaviors, concerned enough to cause a commotion, to express concern, would have been a good thing. We shied away from talking with them directly about some of these things because we didn't want to put them in the middle of a conflict with their mom and stepdad, but I think that was the wrong decision. We needed to be their advocates as well as deal with their other parents, and I think we failed them there.

One time I did try to intervene. Donna was in a car wreck with other kids. I'm sure they were partying pretty hard. Of course, she denied this. The car went off an embankment and Donna got all banged up. No one was cited by the authorities. They didn't even test these kids. This is where I was the isolated person, in part because of my medical background and in part because I said to Brian, "Donna needs treatment." He thought I was an alarmist, which often happens with stepparents. I finally convinced him that I was serious and that her life was at risk, and we went together to talk with Adele and Danny. They believed that I was making a mountain out of a molehill. Brian kind of backpedaled. I felt like the lone wolf. Again looking back, I had some clinical instincts that were right. Donna went on to have some significant substance abuse problems as an adult. There have been many other such situations, and they continue to this day, where I am the alarmist in Brian's eyes, where I am the dramatist. But the girls needed more guidance and intervention, and I do think we failed them in that, even though we did help them to grow up feeling loved and treasured.

Reflections

Many of my good teachers in medical school made me aware that the patient is the vulnerable one. As a doctor in training, you can be scared and insecure and all wrapped up in yourself, but you have to remember that it is the patient that is in crisis. It is the same with children. Adults have certain core strengths they can draw on to rise to the occasion, whatever the occasion is. It's the kids who don't have those yet. It would have been an unhappy thing if my stepdaughters had not accepted me, but I'm a grown-up and I know how to deal with unhappy things. They were the vulnerable ones. If we hadn't had them first and foremost in our minds, they would have been the ones who suffered. That's the main thing. With children, you really can't afford to be self absorbed.

For example, early on, I was briefly interested in having my own child. I remember Brian telling me, "I don't think that would be good for Christie and Donna." He was right. Almost as soon as he said it, the thought was over for me because I realized what was important. It might have been different if I had brought children into the relationship. We can only speculate. I think it would have been harder on my relationship with my stepdaughters because I would have had that natural bond with my own biological child. But as far as having a child together after the fact, it might have made the girls feel excluded. And our focus needed to be on them. We moved to be near them. And they knew we were there for them. There was no other reason for us to be there.

We wanted the girls to feel safe and loved and have as little conflict brewing among the adults as possible. I remember saying things on purpose to show my respect for Adele in front of the kids. I still do that. I feel attracted to her as a person, a friend. I have told the kids how much I think of her. Adele and I never competed with each other. Last Christmas we sat next to each other the whole time at our family Christmas gathering. We have a lot to talk about in our work and our interests. We're not deep friends, but we are friends. It is so clear to me that she is the mom. I've never tried to be the mom. Adele let me into Christie's and Donna's lives, which was a great privilege.

Today Christie has two daughters, and Donna has three sons. Their sense of long-term commitments is huge. I'm so happy that their children welcome me as a grandmother. I look forward to my upcoming retirement when I can see these five far-flung grandchildren more often and get to know them even better as individuals.

But we've already been very involved grandparents, being present at each birth, going to family summer camps together, and more.

As much as I love my stepdaughters fiercely and they're totally family to me, I know I don't have the same bond with them that Brian and their mom have. I didn't give birth to them, and I didn't raise them as little children. When the girls have troubles, I see my husband lose sleep and I see Adele withdraw. Adele and Brian both feel so terribly worried by the girls' challenges. I have a slightly more philosophical acceptance and practical attitude. I don't think this is my personality or that I have any better insight or wisdom. I think I would be as paralyzed and demoralized as Brian and Adele if the problem were about my mother or brothers, for instance. So I think the parental bond is different and it needs to be respected. My job is not just to love my stepdaughters but also to support Brian and Adele—because it's really hard and tender to be a parent.

Paul's Story

Paul married Carol when he was eighteen, and they had two daughters, Bobbie and Alex. They divorced about four years later. When he was almost twenty-nine, he moved in with Angelina and her two children, a boy and a girl, Ted and Kyla. Together they had a daughter, Mary. They lived together for about five years before they split up.

What does family mean to you?
My biological family fell apart when I was really young. I include in the concept of family the people I really care about and the people who are really close to me, regardless of the actual relationship.

Growing up
When I was growing up, my mother was incredibly depressed and rarely got out of bed. When I was a little kid, maybe six or seven, I did all the laundry and the shopping. I can remember learning how to get to the store with a note, and then I'd drag the stuff back to the house. I had to figure out how to get myself and my mother through the day. It was hell. I remember going over to my mother's parents' house and things seemed much more normal than at my house. My grandparents died when I was about seven, which was when things really went south.

My dad supported us financially, but he tried not to be

home. I think he had a lot of girlfriends, just my guess, because my mother was constantly freaking out about stuff. I never had much of a relationship with him. He never showed me how to do stuff, so I had to learn on my own and it was pretty hellish sometimes. I remember going out to play baseball, not knowing the rules and being so embarrassed. I had to fake it and just watch for clues as to how everything was going on so I could be normal. I didn't have any male role models until I was older.

I never had friends over to my house. They only got as far as the hallway because things were so dysfunctional. I think some of my friend's parents got it. I can remember them fawning over me a little bit and how good that felt. Maybe that was normal and I thought it was excessive because I didn't have anything to compare it to. Holidays were always tragic. There were always presents and a Christmas tree of some sort, but it was always just lousy. I still dread the holidays.

I grew up in a transitional neighborhood that had been German and French and became primarily African American. My family was one of four that stayed in the neighborhood. I got to hang out with a lot of kids in African American families. There was just so much warmth and so much life in those families that I often wished that I had been black and was part of one of those families. They always seemed very close and very warm.

I remember standing out in front of the first black storefront church and being amazed at the craziness and the music. Loving it. One day I was there with a friend, and at the end of the service, the ladies said, "Come on in." They gave us milk and donuts, and then we were there at every service. They were always inviting us in, and we became part of the whole deal.

When I was sixteen, I left home and pretty much lived on the street. I had been planning to leave since I was little, hoping to find something, to feel better. My whole life, when things got tough, I would move to whatever presented itself to me. There's an opportunity and you just jump ship. Street life is dangerous day to day. I got into a lot of trouble. I was lucky because I was white. I'd be dead if I had been black. People gave me a pass many times where they wouldn't have given a black kid a pass.

I always had menial jobs. In Buffalo when things were good there was a lot of work. I would often go to casual labor offices where drunks and bums showed up at six a.m. for work. I'd work for a day or two and then get a new job. I loved the experience. It was good for me and I learned so much. All my jobs were blue collar, actually no collar. The concept of career has always been alien to me. It doesn't click. This is the disenfranchised way. Not having a path really. Stuff just happens.

Throughout this time I continued to go to high school, but it was constant conflict. I was always suspended. But I won a Regents' Scholarship, one of only three in the school. Despite this, it was hard to gain confidence because growing up I had no one to teach me. I also had a lot of anger, and when the principal handed me my diploma, I was chewing gum. The principal asked me to take the gum out and I put it on the podium. After high school, I went for a minute to a community college but I got bored and left. I never had staying power. Later I went to several schools and finally graduated with a degree in communications.

I wound up seeing a therapist, who basically saved my life. I was writing poetry at the time, and he asked if I wanted to volunteer at the local counseling center. I don't know how I managed to do that because I was such a mess, but I led a poetry workshop and a mural group for gang members and drug addicts. It was easy for me to empathize with them. I worked as a counselor really well because I knew how to get into people's feelings. For me it was survival. I had to understand how people were functioning in the world and what was going on in their heads so I could fake it.

Meeting my first wife, Carol

I met Carol at a teen club in Buffalo when I was about seventeen. Her family seemed much more stable then mine. Her house felt like an upper-class place when in reality her father was a machinist. I remember feeling, "Wow, I wish I could live this way."

When I was almost eighteen and she was sixteen, I sold my motorcycle and we moved to New York and got married. Her family flipped out. We found it extremely hard to make it in New York. We were really alone, and then Carol found out she was pregnant with our first daughter, Bobbie. We were much too young to be pregnant, but after the baby was born, Carol got pregnant a second time with Alex. We didn't know anything. What does being married even mean? "I don't know. Oh we're pregnant." Eventually we moved back to Buffalo and lived with Carol's parents for a short time. We were married for about four years, separated several times and then divorced.

After the divorce, I had the kids on weekends and Carol had them the rest of the time. Having the kids was a great way to meet girls because girls really like a guy with kids. Kids can be a bundle to deal with, so having a girlfriend to help me was good. I loved the kids, but the responsibility of taking care of them wore on me. I was wild and out of control. I had no clue. I would go to school for a semester and then drop out. Carol resented that because she had these kids to take care of. Her anger was legitimate. She was the responsible person, and I respected her for that. I know I have been fortunate. The women I have been with have been good. That's just luck.

This may be an important concept: When you're disenfranchised, the rules that people talk about don't apply to you. You don't even consider them. You move from one thing to the next. It might be good or it might be bad. You keep on moving, hopefully forward.

Meeting Angelina

When I was twenty-nine, I met Angelina at a costume party. She was eight or nine years older and incredibly beautiful. I remember that I was dressed as a medieval character and Angelina was dressed as a Gypsy. She actually is a Gypsy, so she was being herself only more outrageous. I went home with her that night and slept on a couch. Nothing seemed odd, just normal and natural. I can still remember how excited Angelina's young daughter Kyla was when she saw my costume. Today she tells me that I am her knight because the first time she saw me I was in that costume.

Angelina also had a son Ted, and when I met him he was eight and Kyla was seven. The kids had different fathers. They literally never knew their fathers because they disappeared, truly disappeared. Angelina made good money and didn't need them. She worked at General Motors and always made more money than I did. This was a lady who could really take care of business, and she was also the most eccentric person I have ever known. It didn't take long before we moved in together, just a couple of weeks. Angelina and I never got married because I was always too peripatetic. If I had a chance to go somewhere I would go, which was okay with her.

Angelina's family was like the family I never had. Her dad died in Puerto Rico when she was really young, and later her mom married an Italian guy. I loved him. He grew grapes and made wine in the backyard. We would sit and sip whisky on his front porch for hours. Her mom loved to cook, and I loved to eat her cooking. Angelina's family was extended with lots of lots of brothers and sisters. It was beautiful.

I got along well with Angelina's kids, but then I get along with kids and animals really well anyway, just not so well with adults. Some people say, "You did a nice thing being a father to her children, a wonderful thing." But what else would you do? I'm here. The kids are cool. I'm having fun. They're having fun. Sometimes they're stupid kids and we get into a fight. That's pretty normal. Kyla was easy to deal with. Ted was a boy. I understood his rebellion, just normal stuff. If their fathers had been around probably there would have been a different dynamic. A lot of it had to do with Angelina. I think of myself as someone who is open and gentle. I think she saw me as that and trusted me with the kids. Angelina made a magical environment. It was a love-filled house but also crazy. She was kooky in a lot of ways, but the kids were open and loving. All I had to do was be open and loving back.

Angelina and I never talked about parenting styles or philosophies. I don't think there is any mystery about raising kids, other than having patience and keeping yourself from losing your mind. I had no models. Maybe that helped. It really set the stage for everything and maybe that's why it was easier for me with the kids. I didn't have any preconceived ideas. I was the calming person in that household.

About a year and a half after we met, Angelina and I had our own child, Mary. We didn't overtly plan on having a child but it was obviously a possibility since she wasn't using birth control. We were really excited. I was way more together than I was with my first kids. Angelina's kids loved having the baby. At first it was okay with my kids, later things got worse.

Problems with Carol, my ex-wife

When I first met Angelina, I was excited about her lifestyle and wanted to include my girls in that. When our kids first met each other things were just normal, a little shyness just like any kids meeting new kids. But within about six months after moving in with Angelina, things began to get ugly with Carol. It began with something innocent. Ted was climbing a tree, and I encouraged my daughter Bobbie to also climb. She was really athletic, and I knew she could climb as well as Ted. Once I found her climbing up a refrigerator. Bobbie must have come home upset and told her mom that something had happened. It was probably a very normal misunderstanding, but Carol seemed to blow it up into this huge thing. Carol and I never talked about it, but the next time I came over to pick up the kids she said, "Why did you make Bobbie do that? She didn't want to do that." This was something concrete that Carol needed to keep me from seeing the girls, something she could hold on to. Carol was really angry at me and wouldn't let go.

After that, things became much more difficult. Carol began to alienate me from the kids. This was the first time in my life that I was alienated from my kids. I had the legal right to see Bobbie and Alex during weekends but every time I would go over to their house to pick them up, it was a little strange and uncomfortable. The kids didn't want to come back to Angelina's house because Angelina's kids were there, and Carol had told the kids that Mary was part of the "other family." When they didn't want to go with me, Carol would say, "You don't have to go if you don't want to." I would tell them, "I've got tickets to go to the amusement park this weekend," and they would ask, "Are Kyla and Ted going?" I realized that it was about Angelina's kids. How else could Carol turn my kids against me? I had always gotten along with my daughters. Before that incident, the kids would come home happy. We always had fun together. I'm convinced that Carol made my daughters think that I chose the other kids over them. Carol poisoned the relationship. She said that I cared more about Angelina's kids than my own. They felt threatened by the fact that I had other kids.

Angelina's kids never got to the point where they could be close to my kids because after the tree incident it was tense all the time. Angelina's kids wanted to know about my kids and would ask questions: What are they doing? Where do they go to school? It was really hard because I had so little contact with my kids during that time. That period was horrid. The worst lasted about three or four years. If things were in color, then that period was in sepia.

I worked really hard to keep my relationship with my kids. I never abandoned the situation. As hard as it was, I never gave up. I would be on the phone wanting to know what was going on in their lives, showing that I wanted contact even if the contact wasn't quality. When I traveled I always sent packages, not very expensive stuff, but these little, cheap, cool things. I always bought my kids Easter baskets, but one year they sat in my house for like a month because I couldn't give them to the girls. I felt awful every time I saw those baskets. I can still see them sitting on the porch. I thought to myself, "Okay, I just have to get through this somehow without making it worse than it is." I could not possibly lose the connection with my kids.

Angelina was always supportive of me, but there was no chance she could intercede. Angelina and Carol never talked. She would have been a partner with Carol, but Carol wouldn't ever be a partner with Angelina. Angelina was fine with my kids coming over and never understood why Carol wouldn't want their father to be involved in their lives. She would have killed for that. Neither of her kids had their fathers. The thing that kills me is that I don't know anyone who doesn't love Angelina. If my kids could have just stepped into her world long enough to be caught up in it, it would have been a whole different experience because it was fun being there. The neighbors, everyone, came over to Angelina's house. It was Grand Central Station. It was too bad, but my kids never had a relationship with Angelina.

Carol and I couldn't talk about the problems. She was more than angry. She felt sheer hatred toward me. Things became so intense, explosive, and ugly. The worst of it lasted for about four years. For a while I wondered if this was because of the breakup of our marriage. I had been an idiot. I did ruin our marriage. If I had had a better relationship with Carol, everything would have been different. There might have been a sense of normalcy and continuity. I have learned that if you can't cement the relationship with the mom, make sure you do everything you can to hang on to the relationship with your kids. That is primary.

My problems with Carol led me to start a men's rights group with Bob, a psychologist I knew. I don't remember the precise genesis of this, but we found that we were both locked out from our kids. Bob was gay. He had been married and wanted to see his kids, but at that time it was impossible. He came to me and said, "You know I've been finding more and more men like us. What do you think about starting a group?" So we did. We'd sit down as a group and talk. We tried to come up with strategies. We even hooked up with a lawyer for advice. We'd meet weekly and any given week there were five to eleven men. Some of the men deserved to be locked out. If you don't pay child support you should be locked out. Everyone wanted more access to their kids, and the courts at that time just didn't give men too much room. To me it seemed the system was stacked against men.

Breaking up with Angelina

After about five years, Angelina and I split up. It was pretty intense at Angelina's house, and I needed some distance. I didn't move far, maybe a block or so from her house so that any time anyone needed me, I was right there. Her kids thought of me as their dad. I saw Angelina and the kids most days of the week, and we stayed in each other's business all the time. My relationship with Angelina has been crazy at times but also wonderful, and there was never any question that we wouldn't continue to see each other.

Angelina eventually moved to Detroit, Michigan, to live with a man she had known before who was begging her to come live with him. He is a great guy and I respect him Kyla and Mary went with her and Ted stayed in Buffalo. He was old enough to live on his own. I'm not jealous of Angelina's partner, but things would go through my brain like, "He's usurping my territory with Mary." She was about nine when they moved. I went all the time to visit her and talked with her every day on the phone. Today Mary considers him to be her child's grandfather. He's Grandad and I'm Poppi.

Reuniting with my daughters

When my daughters were teenagers, Carol moved to New Orleans with Alex, and Bobbie came to live with me. I had to rebuild my relationship with her. It was hard because she was pretty wild and crazy. I used to go to about a dozen hip bars in the city. That was my scene. Sometimes the bar owners would call and say, "Your daughter is here. I know she is not of age, what should we do?" I made Bobbie promise not to drink and drive, and to remind her, I bought a poster with some horrible photo to put up in her room.

I would often visit Alex in New Orleans, but I didn't really connect with her until she moved to San Francisco. It was magical because we really clicked. She was living in some crazy apartment in a really old building. I can still bring that room into focus because the experience was so intense for me. She wanted to play songs for me on her guitar. This was so wonderful. I had wanted this all my life, to be this close. She reached out to me and

I accepted it. Since then things have been much better.

It's still hard to talk with Bobbie and Alex about what happened. The story that they tell themselves is that their mother and I were so young when we got married, that it was doomed. That's how they perceive it, which I think is pretty healthy. I don't disagree with them at all. I could skate on that. The story I tell myself is that I wasn't there all the time when they were growing up. In the beginning I was not a good father in the sense that I was out on the streets. I was a goofball. I have a lot of guilt. But now I feel so fortunate that things are pretty good.

My children and stepchildren as adults

My children are doing better than I did. I still have no clue about what I'm doing. They all seem to have goals and pretty solid lives. Bobbie is working in a field that isn't secure, but she is putting money in the bank and doing things that will help her future. Alex is married to a very successful man. She is really, really careful not to let anything untoward go on in her life. Everything is controlled, including raising her daughter. Everything is so meticulous. It's mind-blowing to me. Bobbie has some of the same stuff, but she is a lot more adventurous, like me. Mary has lots of her mom in her. She is comfortable around people and natural. I'm impressed with how she conducts her life, but sadly she has almost no relationship with my other daughters. One of my goals is to bring them together, and I'm really happy that Alex and Mary are talking now. One thing I am proud of is that my daughters have a sense of morality, a really strong sense of morality. They're not going to cheat anyone. I feel so good about that. I am that way too.

After Angelina moved to Atlanta, my relationship with

my stepdaughter Kyla did not continue as strongly, but when we see each other she still refers to me as the only dad she ever knew. Ted is more reticent, a withdrawn musician type. He has a chip on his shoulder, and I know that's because his father split. Neither one ever had a relationship with their father. It breaks my heart. I remember one time Kyla's father was in town and he called to say he wanted to see Angelina. Kyla was so excited, but he never showed. It was just so horrible. Ted and Kyla will stay in my life forever, and I can't picture not being connected with Angelina forever.

Reflections

What are your expectations as a parent and stepparent? Learn to love your stepkids. Get to know them. Enjoy them. It's a blast.

One thing I have learned is to defer to the mom. When things got nitty gritty, I would defer to Angelina. In the back of my mind I thought, if crap really hits the fan, she will take the brunt of it. It made my relationship with her kids easier because I didn't have a whole lot of my ego invested in it. They weren't my kids, so this was not a reflection of me. If I could just have a good relationship and a good time, it was fine. As a stepdad, I could kind of remove myself a little bit. With Mary, Bobbie and Alex, my own kids, the ego thing is real. Even though I really want everyone to do well, if Ted screws up it doesn't stick me in the heart. It's not as intense. Maybe this is a biological thing.

My advice to fathers who are alienated from their kids is this: Just hang in there. Never give up. There may be nothing you can do about your relationship with their mom, but you do have an option to keep up the relationship with your kids. Don't let the connection with your kids be broken. You will regret it for the rest of your life.

Lessons Learned

I have learned that for many people it is really hard to be a stepparent. Granted, it is also hard to be a parent, but it is much harder to be a stepparent. It just is. If it weren't, the divorce rate for second marriages with children would not be so high, 70 percent. The stepparents in the book have talked about some of the reasons. The relationships are complicated. There are minefields pretty much everywhere. In the words of Sarah, "Stepfamilies do not begin on a stable footing."

On the other hand, I have also learned that as hard as it is to be a stepparent, there are many who figure out how to be pretty good at it. But this doesn't just happen. It takes effort, patience and a whole lot of planning, the same things you need for your biological kids, but much more so. But it can and does happen. If not, what explains the 30 percent of stepfamilies that do stay together? What follows is a summary of some of the most important things the stepparents in this book want you to know about how to be included in the 30 percent.

1. **Ask yourself, "Do I really want to do this?"** This may be the most important question you ask yourself. Is this for me? Can I parent another person's child? Just because you love kids does not mean you will love your stepchild. Just because you love your new spouse does not mean you will love their children, or that their children will love you. Go into this with your eyes wide

open, and be as clear as possible about your expectations. Think long and hard, and if you are not sure, you might want to reconsider. Remember John's words, "If you are not sure, I could see how this could be a great strain on a relationship. It takes a special kind of person to be a successful stepparent."

2. **Make your marriage a top priority.** A great relationship may not be enough to get you through the challenges you will face as a stepparent, but I can assure you that without it, you are in big trouble. For many stepparents this can be challenging because, unlike your first time around, you are so busy with work and kids, that it seems impossible to find the time.

So here is what you need to do. You need to make a concerted effort to find time to be alone, just the two of you, on a regular basis. And you must hold on to that time. Tell everyone you know, "This is our time." Mark and Fran had their Wednesday nights. As Mark said, "Our Wednesday nights became sacred to us. That's one of the reasons we have such a strong relationship." Fran added, "We were so excited to meet each other as individuals, and that was the time we could be those individuals."

Find *your* version of a Wednesday night. Joan and Harry go away together every other month for a weekend, and every year they return to Chicago where, in Joan's words, they became "us." Harry said, "How can you even know if that person is right for you if your time together is about making sure kids get fed and take baths, and seeing kid movies all the time?"

3. **Involve your kids and stepkids in decisions about the family.** It's important when bringing families

together that you include the kids in discussions about how to make your new family home a welcoming place for *all* the kids, whether they live with you part-time or full-time. Give them lots of choices. Let them help pick out furniture or the color of their room, go shopping with you for food, or pick out a pet. This new home belongs to *everyone.* The point is this—you are creating a new family unit and everyone in it has to feel that they have special things to contribute, that they belong equally.

4. **Clarify your role**. If there were a job description for stepparents, it would read something like this: Wanted--a person who is patient, fair, caring, secure, flexible, not easily hurt or rattled, willing to let go of pretty much everything all the time, and most important, has a really good sense of humor. In other words, a saint. You will need to draw from all these qualities and skills, especially the humor, as you figure out what role you will and will not play.

A good way of thinking about your role is that it is somewhere between an aunt or uncle and a parent. Mark reminded us, "She was Fran and I was Mark. We were the adults, the husband of their mother or the wife of their father, so we were parent-like but not a mother or father. This is a hard line and we were careful not to cross that line." What does parent-like mean? It means that you do most of the things parents do on a daily basis—cook, clean, schlep the kids around, buy them shoes, take them to the doctor, etc. You also remind them to do their homework, make sure they do their chores, and tell them to turn down the music. Fran said, "When the children are with you, these are people that you help take care of. It's the same feeling I have for my own children."

At the same time, the stepparents and parents agree that major disciplining should be left to the real parents. When stepparents take on this role, it can cause huge problems. Recall Beth's story about her husband when early in their marriage, he hit one of her children. In an instant, her trust was gone and her marriage went downhill from there. Harry explained, "There's a different dynamic in high conflict situations with a stepkid that you don't have with your own kid whom you have raised from infancy. This leads to misinterpretations." Nonetheless, this is a hard one for many stepparents because it brings out so many complicated feelings and questions. They may think, "I do so many things for your child, and yet I am locked out when it comes to the big things. Don't you trust me?" Understandable feelings, which is why I included the "willing to let go of pretty much everything all the time" as part of the job description.

5. **Think about what you bring to the table.** Remember that you are not a "Stepford Stepparent." You come with a history, values and interests, and you have important things to offer your stepkids. As Sarah said, "I can't say enough about how important it is to find a little patch of earth that you and your stepkid can share that doesn't belong to anyone else. It is really important for stepparents to present themselves as something different, not better, but someone who brings a different outlook, perspective and opportunities."

Tonia regretted not doing this. Trying not to "rock the boat," she did not encourage her stepdaughters academically, even though education was one of her main values. As she said, "Some of the things we failed to do amounted to a betrayal of the kids, I now believe. For the girls to have understood that they had at least their dad and me really concerned about certain behaviors, concerned enough to cause a commotion, to express concern, would have been a good thing." Remember that even though you are not the "real parent," you have a lot to offer. Find the things you have in common with your stepchildren. Beth bonded with her stepchild through reading and writing, Harry through sports, and Paul by being a big kid himself.

6. **Create open and honest lines of communication.** There is a reason you will see this advice in every self-help book on stepparenting. Open and honest communication between and among the many people in your new family is critical to its success, especially during the first few years. Without it, there is really no hope. Like the stepparents in this book, you will experience a range of emotions, many not so pleasant. You may feel disrespected, unappreciated, angry, hurt, and invisible. Your new spouse may say things about your child you do not want to hear. You may feel things about your stepchild you are not proud of. You may think, "I am the adult here. I can make things work." Only you can't, at least not by yourself. You need to be able to talk about these things with your spouse in an open and honest way, without feeling defensive or judged. I am not saying that this will be easy. But it must be done.

If you need help, find it—other stepparents, a counselor, rabbi, minister or a good friend. And hopefully, as Harry learned, you will move from venting to constructive problem solving. Once Harry made the wise decision to listen, really listen, to his wife, they were able to make some positive changes in their family. The successful stepfamilies found a way to talk about the hard stuff, not just once, but on an ongoing basis. They built this into the very fabric of their relationship. John said, "I have learned how important it is to be able to communicate with each other. You need to be able to build trust with each other." At the end of the day, it's all about trust.

7. **Be patient. Give the family the time it needs to gel.** It's hard enough to adjust to living with your partner, but even harder to living with their kids. Even if you have developed a relationship with your stepchild before getting married, it will take time before the new family gels. And accept that there will be times when you may feel like Joan. "One day I looked around and asked, 'Who are these people?'" Sound familiar? The advice is pretty clear and unambiguous. Expect that. Plan for that. Don't rush the relationships. Let them emerge naturally, in their own time.

8. **Choose your battles wisely.** I can assure you, there will be lots of things your stepchildren will do that will make you tear your hair out (and visa versa). You have two choices. You can go to war over every little thing, which will make you batty, or you can decide which of all the things that drive you crazy are the most important. So here is the deal. Decide what is important to you (remember you are not a Stepford Stepparent). As Sarah put it, "Being a stepparent can be the most important lesson in figuring out what really matters. I'm not going to get my knickers in a twist when my stepkids leave their wet towels on the floor or food in their bedrooms, take cookies into the den, forget to use a coaster, or any of the other crap that I think becomes unnerving to many stepparents. At the end of the day, you are fighting over silly turf."

9. **Create new memories.** When you marry a person

with children, you need to remember that before you entered into their lives, they had another family, another history, another set of traditions and memories. Your job is to create your own history, traditions and memories with your new family. This will not just happen; you have to consciously make it happen. Create new traditions at Christmas as Tonia did, organize picnics at the beach, visits to the zoo, and make sure you eat together as a family whenever possible. Take trips together. It doesn't matter where. It could a camping trip to the mountains, or in your backyard for that matter, or a wild life safari in Africa—the point is to do something together as a new family. This is how you create new memories. As Fran said, "It's material to work with. You sit around and say, 'Do you remember when . . .?'"

I leave you with these final thoughts. I am lucky. I love my stepchildren and they love me. My son loves his stepfather and he loves my son. Maybe it's just blind luck. Maybe we did a few things right. I am not sure. But I do know one thing. Like everyone I interviewed for this book, Art and I wanted it to work out. That was equally true for our kids, and for the stepkids I interviewed for my first book. They too wanted their stepfamily to be successful.

And so this leaves me with hope. When people have good intentions, anything is possible. It isn't that I am so naïve that I don't understand the challenges. I can assure you that, like the stepparents in the book, I had my share. It's that I understand the possibilities. I know what can happen when you stick it out, work things through, and get to the other side. You, too, can find yourself sitting around the dinner table with your kids, stepkids and grandkids telling old war stories about "the good old days." Like every other relationship in your life, this one is a dance, albeit an intricate dance, and each of us has to find our own rhythm.

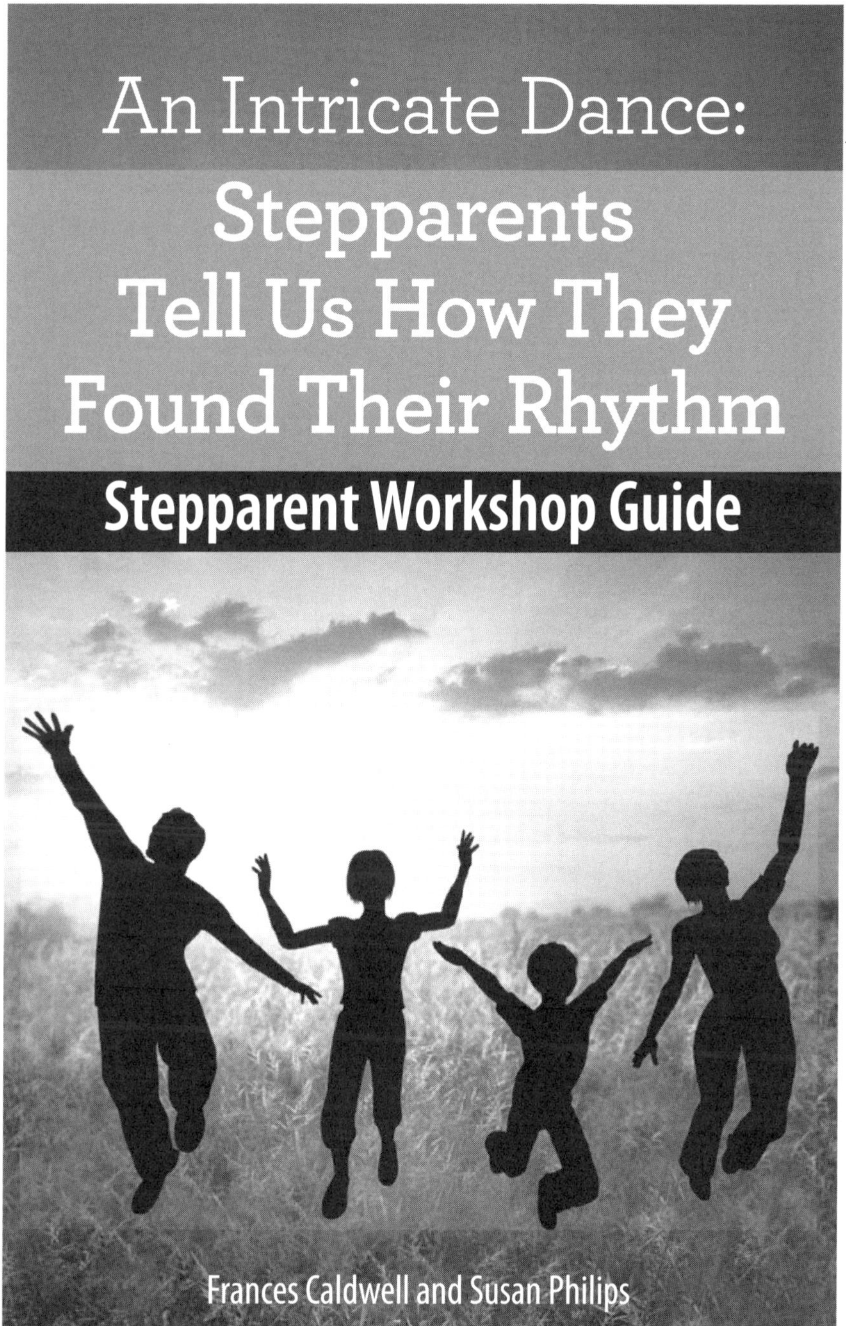
An Intricate Dance:
Stepparents
Tell Us How They
Found Their Rhythm
Stepparent Workshop Guide
Frances Caldwell and Susan Philips

Stepparent Workshop Guide

Notes to the Facilitator

The main goal of this workshop is to help stepparents flourish in their role. This includes both those who are about to take the plunge, and those currently steeped in it. It is not a therapy group, but rather a forum in which stepparents can explore solutions to the problems they face every day. It is organized into nine sessions, each relating to a different piece of advice or lesson learned by the stepparents in this book. It is not necessary to have read the book, but it is recommended. Each session includes an overview to be shared with the participants, a listing of materials you will need, large and small group activities, and a homework assignment where participants apply what they have learned to their stepfamily. Every session begins by reviewing the homework assignment.

You don't have to be a therapist to lead this workshop. Anyone with a desire to help stepparents can do this, including rabbis, ministers, counselors, and even stepparents themselves. You might even try it with just you and your partner. The workshop can as easily be held in a living room as in a classroom. Wherever you decide to hold it, we advise you to set up an atmosphere that is informal, warm, and friendly. Set up chairs in a circle or have participants sit around a table. Food is a great icebreaker, so try to serve something at every session. Participants could help with this. Name tags also help, especially the first session.

We know that people have busy lives, so we have tried to create a model that is as flexible as possible. While the sessions are sequenced, you should feel free to adapt them to meet the needs of your group. This goes for time as well. The sessions are designed to last for an hour, but some may go on for more time and some for less. As a facilitator, gauge your group. We would, however, encourage you to be open to what teachers refer to as a "teachable moment." If your group is hotly engaged in a discussion, let it continue.

Prepare a schedule that lists session topics, dates, and times and hand it out at your first session. You might also want to talk with the group about setting up some ground rules. You want to make sure participants feel safe and secure in the group and everyone has an opportunity to contribute.

One last thing. Remember the purpose of the workshop is less about venting and more about problem-solving. Yes, you want to provide an opportunity for people to express their feelings, and yes, this can be very emotional, but remember that the goal of the workshop is to help stepparents flourish in their role. So make sure that you turn the emotion into practical solutions. That is the key here.

Session 1
Getting to Know Each Other

Overview:
This session is an opportunity for participants to get to know each other a little. Chances are there will be both those who are contemplating marrying someone with children and those who are already living in a stepfamily but need some help in making it work.

Materials:
None

Activity:
1. Read the Overview.
2. This activity has three rounds. Going around the circle have participants respond to the following questions:

   Round A - Tell us who you are. Ask participants to provide their first names and how many stepchildren or potential stepchildren they have or will have, as well as how many of their own children they have. Have them add why they think they need this workshop and what they would like to learn.

   Round B - Tell us how you define *family* and describe the kind of family you come from. A person's idea of family definitely affects their expectations for a new family. It's a good idea for participants to examine their own expectations. Ask: What does the word *family* mean to you? Has your definition of family changed over the years? If you feel comfortable, describe what it was like growing up.

   Round C - Tell us what you think you bring to a

stepfamily. What are the assets you have that you can share? Everyone has something special to offer their stepfamily—skills, talents, interests, hobbies, and experiences. Have them think about what they can contribute.

3. Ask participants to use one word to describe how they are feeling at this moment about being a stepparent.

Homework:

Ask participants to spend some time with their spouses or significant others talking about family. What kind of family did they grow up in, how do they define family, and what does family mean to them? Are their feelings about family relatively the same or are there major differences? If there are differences, think about how they might impact the new family.

Session 2
Finding Time to be Together

Overview:
The stepparents in this book told us that in order to have a good relationship with their spouse they needed "alone time." When you marry someone with kids, your life will be filled with all kinds of new obligations and responsibilities. You may feel that you are "in over your head," and to boot, you may ask yourself: When will I have time alone with my new spouse? Figuring out that answer may be one of the most important things you can do. In this activity, participants will come up with a realistic plan to spend time alone with their spouse, without kids.

Materials:
Paper and pencils/pens

Homework Review:
Ask each participant to discuss briefly what they did.

Activity:
1. Read the Overview.
2. Ask participants to brainstorm on paper things they can do with their spouse. The paper should have three columns, one for each day, each week and each year. Tell them to include simple things like taking a walk and big things like traveling to Paris.
3. Ask them to choose one activity from each list and write what they will need to make these things happen: money, babysitters, time, schedules, etc. Ask them to write down problems that might come up and how they will deal with them? How will this

impact their custody arrangement? How will their kids react? Other things?

4. Have them pair up with one other participant and review their ideas.
5. Bring everybody back together as a group. Ask each participant to choose one thing from their list and tell how they will make it happen.

Homework:

Ask participants to share their lists and ideas with their partners and begin to make a plan. Tell them they can build as they go along.

Session 3
Involving Kids in Decisions—
A Museum Walk

Overview:

When you bring together families, it is important to provide ample opportunities for kids and stepkids to participate in the decision-making process. They need to feel that they have a voice in things that impact their lives, from the color of their new room to what they eat for lunch. In this session, participants will identify a list of creative ways to involve their kids and stepkids in their new family.

Materials:

Butcher paper
Marking pens

Homework Review:

Ask each participant to discuss briefly what they did.

Activity:

1. Read the Overview.
2. Break the group into four smaller groups, each around one of the following areas where decisions need to be made as a family: meals, entertainment, home decorating, household chores. Give each group a large sheet of butcher paper and a marker. Make sure each group has a different color marker.
3. Give participants the following directions:
   Brainstorm all the different ways you could include your kids and stepkids in decisions, and how you might adapt them to different age groups.
   Write them on the butcher paper and hang the paper

on the wall.

4. Tell participants to move around the room in their group, looking at other groups' idea sheets. Ask them to add their own ideas to the paper using their group's color marker. Allow 3 to 5 minutes at each sheet and tell them to move on to the next one until they have added their ideas to all four sheets
5. Bring the groups back together as one large group. Ask a representative from each group to review their list.
6. Discuss with the group how to do the kind of activity they have just completed with their families. How will they adapt it?

Homework:

Ask participants to try this activity with their family.

Session 4
Setting Goals: In our family, we will....

Overview:
The beginning period of any marriage is challenging, but even more so in a stepfamily. Why? Everything is different. Everything is new. In this session, participants will come up with a set of goals to help their new family set a sound foundation.

Materials:
Butcher paper
Markers

Homework Review:
Ask each participant to discuss briefly what they did.

Activity:

1. Read the Overview.
2. Ask participants to discuss why it is important to set stepfamily goals. Another way to ask this question is this: What happens when you don't?
3. Break the group into smaller groups. Give each group a piece of butcher paper. Ask them to write down at least five goals for their new stepfamily. Using the following prompt: In our stepfamily, we will . . .
4. Encourage the groups to include goals centered on communication, problem solving, manners, household chores, decision making, etc.
5. Bring the group back together and ask each small group to post their sheet on the wall and read their five goals to the large group.
6. Ask them: Which goals are the most important? Are any unrealistic?

7. Ask participants how they will involve everyone in their family in this activity, including small children?

Homework:

Ask each participant to have a goal-setting discussion with their family.

Session 5
Clarifying your Role

Overview:

Parent-like is a term used by several of the stepchildren in *Stepchildren Speak* and by stepparents in this book as well to describe the appropriate role for a stepparent. But what does *parent-like* mean? One thing is clear; all stepparents must decide for themselves what their role will be. In this workshop, participants will begin to define their own stepparent role.

Materials:

Butcher paper
Markers
Paper and pencils/pens

Homework Review:

Ask each participant to discuss briefly what they did.

Activity:

1. Read the Overview.
2. Break the group into pairs and ask them to list what they think the responsibilities of a stepparent might be. Then have them list the responsibilities they think might belong to the parents (your spouse and the other parent). On a third list have them write those responsibilities they are not sure about.
3. Bring the group back together. Post three large pieces of butcher paper labeled as follows: Stepparent, Parents, and Not Sure.
4. Ask each pair to share their lists with the larger group. Write their responses on the appropriate piece of butcher paper, numbering them. Place

a check by those given more than once. Identify the points of agreement and disagreement.

5. Ask participants: Has this session changed how you see your role?

Homework:

In a journal-like entry, ask participants to write how each sees his/her role as a stepparent and discuss it with their spouse.

Session 6
Talking about It

Overview:

There will always be conflicts in families, more so in stepfamilies where there is less trust and people fear that expressing their true feelings will make things worse. This session will provide participants with tools to help them talk about conflicts in their stepfamilies.

Materials:

Talking Guidelines handouts (prepared ahead of time)

Homework Review:

Ask each participant to discuss briefly what they did.

Activity:

1. Read the Overview.
2. Ask the group about how they resolve conflicts in their stepfamilies. Are there strategies they have that have worked?
3. Pass out the Talking Guidelines handout. Read each out loud, stopping to give or ask for examples.

Talking Guidelines:

- **I.** **Be aware of what your body is saying.** Most important of all is eye contact. Also be careful of your facial expressions, making sure your expression and your body language aren't saying something different from your words.
- **II.** **Be non-judgmental.** Avoid accusatory language using the pronoun *you*; instead send *I* messages. Also, choose kind, respectful words.

III. **Get the full story.** Ask questions to get not only the facts but also the underlying feelings. Ask for clarification when you don't understand; repeat what is said to be sure you have it right.

IV. **Keep it real.** Honesty and authenticity should rule the day. Pretending, exaggerating, and getting dramatic only cloud understanding.

4. Divide the large group into two groups. Give the following directions:
   - As a group, choose one of the following problem areas common in stepfamilies: loyalty, money, ex-spouse, jealousy, discipline.
   - Come up with a conflict scenario within the area you have chosen. For example: your husband's ex-wife calls every night at dinner time, or your stepchildren do not bring enough clean clothing when they come for a visit, or your wife complains that you spend too much money on your children.
   - Prepare a short skit that uses the guidelines.
   - Present your skit to the other group.
5. After each skit ask the following question: Referring to the guidelines, what worked and what didn't? What are other strategies for handling the problem?
6. Going around the circle have each person share something from this session they will use with their stepfamilies.

Homework:

Ask participants to teach the Talking Guidelines to their stepfamily. Tell them to be creative and make it fun.

Handout A

Talking Guidelines

Be aware of what your body is saying. Most important of all is eye contact. Also be careful of your facial expressions, making sure your expression and your body language aren't saying something different from your words.

Be non-judgmental. Avoid accusatory language using the pronoun *you*; instead send *I* messages. Choose kind, respectful words.

Get the full stoy. Ask questions to get not only the facts but also the underlying feelings. Ask for clarification when you don't understand; repeat back what is said to be sure you have it right.

Keep it real. Honesty and authenticity should rule the day. Pretending, exaggerating, and getting dramatic only cloud understanding.

Session 7
Choosing Your Battles

Overview:
Not everything has to be a crisis. Most of the stepparents in this book recommend that you pick and choose your battles with your stepchildren carefully. You can't worry about everything they do or say or you'd be a complete wreck and so would your family. Some things you just need to brush off. In this session participants will discuss which things they can brush off and which they cannot.

Materials:
Handouts with List of Behaviors

Homework Review:
Ask each participant to discuss briefly what they did.

Activity:
1. Read the Overview.
2. Ask partipants to discuss he following: Are you the kind of person who can easily brush things off or are you a "deal with it now" kind of person?
3. Provide each participant with a list of behaviors as follows (feel free to modify or add to the list) and briefly go over this handout with the group.

Your stepchild . . .

a) forgets to bring the new coat you bought her back from her mother's house
b) doesn't want to go to religious services with the family.
c) slams his bedroom door.
d) while she stays at your house, calls

the other parent several times a day.

e) doesn't want to come to your house because it hurts her mother.
f) answers a phone call and forgets to put the dishes away.
g) comes home late from a party without calling.
h) says something bad about you to a friend and you overhear.
i) says, "Don't tell me what to do."
j) leaves dirty towels on the floor after showering.
k) doesn't want to spend time with your children.
l) overhears you say something critical about his father and storms out of the house.

4. In small groups have participants discuss the list of behaviors. Which are insignificant enough to be brushed off? Which are not? There will be varied opinions, so consensus is not necessary.
5. Bring the groups back into the large group. Ask the following questions to generate more discussion:

- Did anyone find that none of the behaviors could be brushed off?
- Which ones are the least worrisome?
- Of all the behaviors, which have the potential to escalate? Why?
- Which ones would cause you to consult with your spouse or partner?
- Are there any you would leave entirely up to the real parents? Why?
- What have you learned about yourself in this session?

Homework:

List the "battles" you are facing or fear you will face in the future and number them in order of importance.

Handout B

List of Behaviors

Your stepchild . . .

a. forgets to bring the new coat you bought her back from her mother's house
b. doesn't want to go to religious services with the family.
c. slams his bedroom door.
d. while she stays at your house, calls the other parent several times a day.
e. doesn't want to come to your house because it hurts her mother.
f. answers a phone call and forgets to put the dishes away.
g. comes home late from a party without calling.
h. says something bad about you to a friend and you overhear.
i. says, "Don't tell me what to do."
j. leaves dirty towels on the floor after showering.
k. doesn't want to spend time with your children.
l. overhears you say something critical about his father and storms out of the house.

Session 8
Creating New Memories as a Stepfamily – "Do you remember when…"

Overview:
Memories are the glue that holds many families together. It seems we never tire of telling the same stories or looking through the same photo albums. They document our shared history. When two families come together to create a stepfamily, they are a blank slate. They have no history together, no funny stories or no vacation photos. Tell participants they need to create and document their *new* momories. In this session, they will brainstorm ways to do this.

Materials:
3 by 5 cards
Pencils/pens

Homework Review:
Ask each participant to discuss briefly what they did.

Activity:
1. Read the Overview.
2. Give each participant a 3 by 5 card. Ask them to complete the sentences:

- My most favorite memory growing up is . . .
- I love that memory because . . .

3. Ask participants to put their cards in a large bowl. Then have each participant pick one from the bowl and read it out loud. When everyone has read one, ask: What do these memories have in common?
4. Break the group into pairs. Explain that each person will help the other come up with ideas about how

to create new memories and how to document those memories. Remind the participants that every stepfamily is different and what might work with one will not with another. First, have them share with each other what their stepfamily enjoys doing together. And then, together think of ways to document these experiences (a special wall of photos, scrapbooks, trophy case, etc.).

5. Bring the large group back together and ask each participant to share one idea from their discussion.
6. Ask participants to compare their favorite memory from childhood with their ideas from this activity.

Homework:

Ask participants to bring their family together and come up with a stepfamily memory they would like to preserve. Then ask them to create a way to document that memory (photo, program, recipe, etc.).

Session 9
Bringing it all together—The Top Ten List

Overview:
Creating a happy stepfamily does not happen overnight. It takes time, and it takes planning. Hopefully these sessions have provided participants with some creative ways to move forward. In this session, participants will create a stepfamily Top-Ten List of the most important things a stepparent should know.

Materials:
Butcher paper, markers, magazines, scissors, glue etc.

Homework Review:
Ask each participant to discuss briefly what they did.

Activity:

1. Read the Overview.
2. Ask participants to think about all the topics covered in the workshop. Going around the circle, ask participants: What is the most important thing you have learned in this workshop about being a stepparent.
3. Provide each participant with a piece of butcher paper. Place the materials (markers, magazines, etc) in the center of the room. Ask participants to write at the top: My Top Ten List of Advice for Stepparents. Ask each to come up with their own list, from most important to least important. Encourage them to use the materials, be creative and have fun.
4. Have participants post their lists on the wall. Ask everyone to walk around and read each person's list.

5. Bring the group back together and have participants turn to the person next to them and offer a wish for that person and a second wish for the whole group.

Homework:
Ask participants to take their list home and share it with their spouse and other stepparents.

To order additional copies of this book or another Susan Philips book, go to

www.aywnpublications.com

or call

503-206-8853.

Photo by
Jacob Pinger,
Susan's son

Susan Philips is the Co-Director of College Path LA, a program to help first generation immigrant students through the college application process. She also consults with LACER Hollywood Stars, an organization that promotes quality after-school programming in arts, literacy and sports in several inner-city middle and high schools. Susan received a Master's Degree in Journalism from the University of Southern California and a teaching credential from the University of California at Irvine. This is her third book. *Stepchildren Speak: 10 Grown-up Stepchildren Teach Us How to Build Healthy Stepfamilies*, a collection of interviews with stepchildren, is her first. *In the Heart of Another: Immigrant Women Tell Their stories,* is her second. Susan lives in Los Angeles.